August . 1946.

To J.W.

with best wishes

from J. D.

THE APOSTOLIC PREACHING

THE APOSTOLIC PREACHING
AND ITS DEVELOPMENTS

THREE LECTURES

WITH AN APPENDIX ON
ESCHATOLOGY AND HISTORY

BY
C. H. DODD

NORRIS-HULSE PROFESSOR OF DIVINITY IN THE
UNIVERSITY OF CAMBRIDGE

LONDON
HODDER & STOUGHTON LIMITED

First Printed 1936

MADE AND PRINTED IN GREAT BRITAIN FOR
HODDER AND STOUGHTON, LTD., BY
HAZELL, WATSON AND VINEY, LTD., LONDON AND AYLESBURY

PREFACE

THE THREE LECTURES contained in this volume were given under the auspices of the University of London, at King's College, London, in the Michaelmas Term, 1935. They are printed substantially as delivered, with only a minimum of revision. I have added as an appendix a paper which was read as a presidential address to the Oxford Society of Historical Theology on October 24, 1935. It will be printed according to custom in the Transactions of the Society. I am grateful to the committee and members of the Society for their consent to this anticipatory publication.

C. H. D.

CAMBRIDGE,
January 9, 1936.

CONTENTS

I

The Primitive Preaching

I

The Primitive Preaching

"IT PLEASED GOD," says Paul, "by the foolishness of the Preaching to save them that believe."[1] The word here translated "preaching," *kerygma*, signifies not the action of the preacher, but that which he preaches, his "message," as we sometimes say.

The New Testament writers draw a clear distinction between preaching and teaching. The distinction is preserved alike in Gospels, Acts, Epistles, and Apocalypse, and must be considered characteristic of early Christian usage in general. Teaching (*didaskein*) is in

[1] 1 Cor. i. 21.

a large majority of cases ethical instruction.[1]
Occasionally it seems to include what we
should call apologetic, that is, the reasoned
commendation of Christianity to persons
interested but not yet convinced. Sometimes, especially in the Johannine writings,
it includes the exposition of theological
doctrine. Preaching, on the other hand, is
the public proclamation of Christianity to the
non-Christian world. The verb *keryssein*
properly means " to proclaim." A *keryx*
may be a town crier, an auctioneer, a herald,
or anyone who lifts up his voice and claims
public attention to some definite thing he

---

[1] Hence the title *Teaching of the Twelve Apostles*. The tract-
ate so called gives instruction in Christian morals and ecclesias-
tical practice. It is *didaché*, not *kerygma*. It would therefore be illegitimate to conclude that the Church represented
by this book was not interested in other aspects of Christianity.
If it had issued a " Preaching of the Twelve Apostles," it
might have had a very different character.

has to announce. Much of our preaching in Church at the present day would not have been recognized by the early Christians as *kerygma*. It is teaching, or exhortation (*paraklesis*), or it is what they called *homilia*, that is, the more or less informal discussion of various aspects of Christian life and thought, addressed to a congregation already established in the faith.

The verb " to preach " frequently has for its object " the Gospel." Indeed, the connection of ideas is so close that *keryssein* by itself can be used as a virtual equivalent for *evangelizesthai*, " to evangelize," or " to preach the Gospel." It would not be too much to say that wherever " preaching " is spoken of, it always carries with it the implication of " good tidings " proclaimed.

For the early Church, then, to preach the Gospel was by no means the same thing as to deliver moral instruction or exhortation. While the Church was concerned to hand on the teaching of the Lord, it was not by this that it made converts. It was by *kerygma*, says Paul, not by *didaché*, that it pleased God to save men.

We have to enquire how far it is possible to discover the actual content of the Gospel preached or proclaimed by the apostles.

First, we may place before us certain recurrent phrases which indicate in brief the subject of the preaching. In the Synoptic Gospels we read of " preaching the Kingdom of God," whether the reference is to Jesus or to His followers. In the Pauline epistles we commonly read of " preaching

Christ." In the Acts of the Apostles both forms of expression are used. The apostles preach " Jesus " or " Christ," or they preach " the Kingdom of God." We may observe that in those parts of Acts where the writer speaks in the first person Paul himself is represented as " preaching the Kingdom of God." We may therefore take it that a companion of Paul regarded his preaching as being just as much a proclamation of the Kingdom of God as was the preaching of the first disciples or of their Master, even though Paul does not himself speak of it in those terms.

Such expressions obviously need a good deal of expansion before we can form a clear idea of what it was that the apostles actually preached. We must examine our documents more closely.

The earliest Christian writer whose works are extant is the apostle Paul, and from him our investigation should begin. There are, however, difficulties in attempting to discover the apostolic Preaching in the epistles of Paul. In the first place, the epistles are, of course, not of the nature of *kerygma*. They are all addressed to readers already Christian, and they deal with theological and ethical problems arising out of the attempt to follow the Christian way of life and thought in a non-Christian world. They have the character of what the early Church called "teaching" or "exhortation." They presuppose the Preaching. They expound and defend the implications of the Gospel rather than proclaim it.

In the second place, if we should find it

possible to infer from the epistles what Paul preached, it would be in the first instance what he calls " my Gospel," and not necessarily the Gospel common to all or most early preachers. For Paul, as we know, claimed a high degree of originality in his presentation of the Gospel, and the claim is clearly justified.

Nevertheless, it is, I believe, by no means a hopeless task to recover from the Pauline epistles some indication at least of the character and content of Paul's preaching, and not only of his distinctive preaching, but of what he preached in common with other Christian missionaries.

To begin with, Paul himself was conscious of a distinction between the fundamental content of the Gospel and the teaching which he based upon it. In 1 Cor. i. 23, ii. 2-6, he recalls that at Corinth he had preached "Christ and Him crucified." He would now like to go on to "speak wisdom among mature persons," and regrets that the Corinthians do not show themselves ready for it.

Again, in 1 Cor. iii. 10 *sqq.*, he distinguishes between the "foundation" which he laid, and the superstructure which he and others build upon it. The reference is no doubt to the "building up" of the life of the Church in all its aspects. But a study of the context will show that what was most particularly in his mind was just this distinction between the fundamental Gospel and the higher wisdom (not to be confused with "the wisdom of men") which can be imparted to those

whose apprehension of the Gospel is sufficiently firm.   The " foundation " is Christ,
or, may we not say, it is the Gospel of
" Christ and Him crucified."   Paul himself,
Apollos, and others developed this fundamental Gospel in various ways. The epistles
represent for the most part this development, or superstructure.   But Paul was well
aware that what gave authority to his teaching was the Gospel which underlay it all.

In 1 Cor. xv. 1 *sqq.* he cites in explicit terms
that which he had preached at Corinth :

" that Christ died for our sins according to
the Scriptures ;

and that He was buried ;

and that He rose again the third day accord-
to the Scriptures ;

and that He was seen of Cephas . . ."

"It was thus," he adds emphatically, "that we preached and thus that you believed." He then goes on to draw out certain implications of these fundamental beliefs, part of which he describes as a " mystery," that is, surely, as belonging to that " wisdom " which should follow upon the apprehension of the preaching of " Christ and Him crucified." We seem, therefore, to have here, down to the very words, which he quotes in order that there may be no misunderstanding, a part at least of what Paul was accustomed to preach as Gospel, clearly distinguished from the theological superstructure of his thought: he proclaimed the facts that Christ died and rose again. As he puts it in writing to the Galatians (iii. 1), Christ was

" openly set forth before their eyes as crucified."

These facts, however, are exhibited in a special light. They happened " according to the Scriptures "—a statement whose significance will become clearer presently. Further, Christ died " *for our sins.*" In other words, according to Gal. i. 4, " He gave Himself for us, to rescue us from the present evil age." As this statement occurs in the exordium of the epistle, where Paul may be supposed, according to his practice, to be recalling ideas familiar to his readers, we may take it that it was in some such terms that he spoke of the significance of the death of Christ when he preached in Galatia. The language implies the Jewish doctrine of the two ages, " This Age," and " the Age to

Come." "The entrances of this Age have been made narrow and painful and toilsome, few and evil and full of dangers, and packed with great labours. For the entrances of the greater Age are spacious and secure and bearing the fruit of immortality" (2 Esd. vii. 12–13). Paul's meaning is that by virtue of the death (and resurrection) of Christ the boundary between the two ages is crossed, and those who believe belong no more to the present evil age, but to the glorious Age to Come.

Again in Rom. x. 8-9, the content of "the word of faith which we preach" is given in the terms : "that Jesus is Lord and that God has raised Him from the dead." Thus the proclamation of the resurrection is also a proclamation of the Lordship of Christ. It is in this sense that it is " the Gospel of the glory of Christ " (2 Cor. iv. 4). Indeed, the attainment of universal lordship was, according to Rom. xiv. 9, the very purpose of Christ's death and resurrection : " It was for this that Christ died and came to life, that He might exercise lordship over dead and living alike."

It is noteworthy that the passage just cited leads almost immediately to a reference to the Judgment to come : " We shall all stand before the tribunal of God " (Rom. xiv. 10) —which is also, according to 2 Cor. v. 10, " the tribunal of Christ." We might fairly have inferred that there was in Paul's mind a fixed association of ideas—resurrection, lordship, judgment—even if he had not explicitly stated that in his preaching of the Gospel he proclaimed a " Day when God judges the secrets of men through Christ Jesus " (Rom. ii. 16).

The kind of language he used in preaching judgment to come may be illustrated from 1 Cor. iv. 5: "Judge nothing before the time, until the Lord comes, who will bring to light the things that darkness hides, and expose the motives of hearts; then each person will receive his meed of praise from God"; and from 2 Cor. v. 10: " We must all stand before the tribunal of Christ, that each may receive what pertains to him through his body, according to what he has done, whether good or evil." It is to be observed that in these passages the fact of judgment to come is appealed to as a *datum* of faith. It is not something for which Paul argues, but something from which he argues; something therefore which we may legitimately assume to have been a part of his fundamental preaching. Judgment is for Paul a function of the universal Lordship of Christ, which He attained through death and resurrection, and His second advent as Judge is a part of the *kerygma*—as Judge, but also as Saviour, for in 1 Thess. i. 9–10 Paul sums up the effect of his preaching at Salonica in the terms : " You turned from idols to God, to serve the living and real God, and to await His Son from heaven, whom He raised from the dead— Jesus, who saves us from the coming Retribution."

The Pauline *kerygma*, therefore, is a proclamation of the facts of the death and

2

resurrection of Christ in an eschatological
setting which gives significance to the facts.
They mark the transition from " this evil
Age " to the " Age to Come." The " Age
to Come " is the age of fulfilment. Hence
the importance of the statement that Christ
died and rose " according to the Scriptures."
Whatever events the Old Testament prophets
may indicate as impending, these events are
for them significant as elements in the coming of " the Day of the Lord." Thus the
fulfilment of prophecy means that the Day
of the Lord has dawned : the Age to Come
has begun. The death and resurrection of
Christ are the crucial fulfilment of prophecy.
By virtue of them believers are already delivered out of this present evil age. The
new age is here, of which Christ, again by

virtue of His death and resurrection, is Lord.
He will come to exercise His Lordship both
as Judge and as Saviour at the consummation
of the Age.

We have now to ask how far this form of
kerygma is distinctively Pauline, and how far
it provides valid evidence for the apostolic
Preaching in general.

Paul himself at least believed that in
essentials his Gospel was that of the primitive apostles ; for although in Gal. i. 11–18
he states with emphasis that he did not derive it from any human source, nevertheless
in the same epistle (ii. 2) he says that he laid
" the Gospel which I preach " before Peter,
James and John at Jerusalem, and that they
gave their approval.   Not only so, but in the
locus classicus, 1 Cor. xv. 1 *sqq.*, he expressly

declares that this summary of the Gospel is
what he had " received " as tradition ; and
after referring to other witnesses to the facts,
including Peter, James, and " all the
apostles," he adds with emphasis, " Whether
I or they, it was thus that we preached, and
thus that you believed."

Further, it should be remembered that in
the Epistle to the Romans Paul is addressing
a Church which looked to other founders,
and a Church which he was anxious to con-
ciliate. We may therefore take it that
wherever in that epistle he appeals to the
data of the Christian faith, he is referring to
that which was common to him and to those
preachers of the Gospel to whom the Church
at Rome looked as founders and leaders.
Those elements therefore of the *kerygma*,

which we have already recognized in Romans, are to be regarded not only as parts of what Paul calls " my Gospel," but as parts of the common Gospel.

Again, the opening verses of the epistle (i. 1–4) have the aspect of a formula which Paul could assume as recognized by his readers. They speak of " the Gospel of God which He announced beforehand through His prophets in holy Scriptures." This Gospel concerned " His Son, who was born of the seed of David according to the flesh ; who was appointed Son of God with power according to the Spirit of holiness from the time of the resurrection of the dead—Jesus Christ our Lord." The language is unlike that of Paul in other places, but it sets forth substantially the same idea

of the resurrection—that it marks the attainment of Christ's lordship, as Son of God with
full powers. What is additional is the
affirmation of the Davidic descent of Jesus—
a guarantee of His Messianic status in which
Paul does not seem to have been particularly
interested, but which he cites here as part of
a recognized formula. I should find it hard
to believe that this Christological formula
was coined by Paul himself. He accepts it
as stating the common Gospel which he and
others preached.

Again in Rom. viii. 31–4 the process of
thought demands that the readers should
accept as axiomatic the propositions that
God "did not spare His own Son,
but delivered Him up for us all"; and
that

" it is Christ Jesus, He who died, and more,
> who was raised,
> who is at the right hand of God,
> who also intercedes for us."

We have once again the sense that a formula is being cited, a formula closely akin to that cited in 1 Cor. xv. 1 *sqq.* It is to be noted that the idea of Lordship is here expressed in the phrase " at the right hand of God," which recurs in Col. iii. 1, Eph. i. 20. As we shall see, this formula is deeply rooted in the *kerygma*, and is ultimately derived from Ps. cx. 1 :

" The Lord said unto my Lord,
> Sit thou at my right hand,
> Until I make thine enemies thy footstool."

This text is cited in Mk. xii. 36 (and the Synoptic parallels), and also (as a whole or in part) in Acts ii. 34-35, 1 Cor. xv. 25, Heb. i. 13, etc. Wherever we read of Christ being at the right hand of God, or of hostile powers being subjected to Him, the ultimate reference is to this passage. In view of the place which Ps. cx. 1 holds in the New Testament, we may safely put it down as one of the fundamental texts of the primitive *kerygma*. Indeed, I can see no adequate reason for rejecting the statement of Mark that it was first cited by Jesus Himself in His public teaching in the Temple. It follows that the use of the title " Lord " for Jesus is primitive. Since Bousset's work *Kyrios Christos*, it has been very widely held that this title was derived from Hellenistic usage, and first applied to Jesus in the Gentile Church. Seldom, I think, has a theory been so widely accepted on more flimsy grounds.[1]

We see emerging the outlines of an apostolic Gospel which Paul believed to be common to himself and other Christian missionaries. As the epistles from which we have quoted belong to the fifties of the first century, they are evidence of prime value for the content of the early *kerygma*. And this evidence is in effect valid for a much earlier date than that at which the epistles themselves were written. When did Paul " receive " the tradition of the death and resurrection of Christ ? His conversion

[1] For an answer to Bousset's theory see Burkitt, *Christian Beginnings*, pp. 44–52 ; Rawlinson, *The New Testament Doctrine of the Christ*, pp. 231–267. This is not to deny the importance of Hellenistic influence in helping to fix the connotation of the term as used in worship and in theology by Greek-speaking Christians.

can, on his own showing, be dated not later than about A.D. 33–34.[1]   His first visit to Jerusalem was three years after this (possibly just over two years on our exclusive reckoning) ; at the utmost, therefore, not more than seven years after the Crucifixion. At that time he stayed with Peter for a fortnight, and we may presume they did not spend all the time talking about the weather. After that he had no direct contact with the primitive Church for fourteen years, that is to say, almost down to the period to which our epistles belong, and it is difficult to see how he could during this time have had any opportunity of further instruction in the apostolic traditions.

[1] See my article on the " *Chronology of the Acts and the Pauline Epistles* " in the Oxford *Helps to the Study of the Bible*, 1931, pp. 195–197.

The date, therefore, at which Paul received the fundamentals of the Gospel cannot well be later than some seven years after the death of Jesus Christ. It may be earlier, and, indeed, we must assume some knowledge of the tenets of Christianity in Paul even before his conversion. Thus Paul's preaching represents a special stream of Christian tradition which was derived from the main stream at a point very near to its source. No doubt his own idiosyncrasy counted for much in his presentation of the Gospel, but anyone who should maintain that the primitive Christian Gospel was fundamentally different from that which we have found in Paul must bear the burden of proof.

It is true that the *kerygma* as we have recovered it from the Pauline epistles is fragmentary. No complete statement of it is, in the nature of the case, available. But we may restore it in outline somewhat after this fashion :

The prophecies are fulfilled, and the new Age is inaugurated by the coming of Christ.

He was born of the seed of David.

He died according to the Scriptures, to deliver us out of the present evil age.

He was buried.

He rose on the third day according to the Scriptures.

He is exalted at the right hand of God, as Son of God and Lord of quick and dead.

He will come again as Judge and Saviour of men.

The apostolic preaching as adopted by Paul may have contained, almost certainly did contain, more than this. Comparison with other forms of the *kerygma* may enable us to expand the outline with probability ; but so much of its content can be demonstrated from the epistles, and the evidence they afford is of primary value.

We now turn to another source of evidence, later than the Pauline epistles, and not so direct, but yet of great importance—the account of the apostolic preaching in the Acts of the Apostles.

The date of this work cannot be fixed closely, but it is perhaps more likely to belong to the nineties than to the eighties or seventies of the first century. The author apparently used to some extent the

liberty which all ancient historians claimed
(after the example of Thucydides), of composing speeches which are put into the
mouths of the personages of the story. It
is therefore possible at the outset that the
speeches attributed to Peter and others, as
well as to Paul, may be free compositions of
the author.

But there are indications that the author
of Acts used his historian's privilege with
considerable restraint. Certainly in the first
volume of his work, which we call the
Gospel according to Luke, he can be proved
to have kept closely to his sources in composing the discourses attributed to Jesus
Christ. And in Acts itself, consider the case
of Paul's two apologies, before the people
(xxii. 1–21), and before Festus and Agrippa

(xxvi. 2–23). They give different accounts of his conversion, both differing from the account of the event given by the historian himself in ch. ix. Why should a writer who elsewhere shows himself to be not indifferent to economy of space and the avoidance of repetition have been at the pains of composing, independently, three different accounts of the same event? In the Third Gospel the occasional occurrence of " doublets " is reasonably accounted for by the hypothesis of various sources. Is it not most natural to conclude that in the case before us the author based the two speeches upon sources different from that which he followed in ch. ix? And if so, is any source more likely than some direct or indirect report of the line which Paul himself followed upon these or similar occasions ?

Again, the speech of Paul to the elders of the Ephesian Church in xx. 18-35 contains so many echoes of the language of Pauline epistles that we must suppose, either that the writer had access to these epistles (which is on other grounds improbable), or that he worked upon actual reminiscence of Paul's speech upon this or some similar occasion. And when we observe that this speech occurs in close proximity to "we"-passages, it is reasonable to suppose that the travelling companion who was responsible for these passages, whether or not he was also the author of the whole work, remembered in general lines what Paul said. We conclude that in some cases at least the author of Acts gives us speeches which are not, indeed, anything like verbatim reports (for the style is too " Lucan " and too un-Pauline for that), but are based upon a reminiscence of what the apostle actually said.

It is therefore not unreasonable to suppose that in the speeches given in the earlier part of Acts, the author may have similarly made use of sources. This becomes the more probable in view of the following facts.

(*a*) Negatively, there are few, if any, ideas or expressions introduced which might arouse suspicion because of their resemblance to writings emanating, like the Acts, from the Gentile Church in the late first century ; nor are there any echoes, even in turns of speech, of the distinctively Pauline theology, though the author, whoever he

3

may have been, must have been associated
with the Pauline wing of the Church.[1]   To
suppose that this is due to deliberate archaism
is to attribute to the author of Acts a modern
view of historical writing.

(*b*) Positively, the speeches in question,
as well as parts of the narrative in which they
are embedded, have been shown to contain
a large element of Semitism.   Nor is this
Hebraism of the kind which results from an

[1] The argument here is in danger of moving in a circle ; for
I shall presently show that there are parallels between these
speeches and the epistles of Paul, and that these are not due
to borrowing from Paul.   But I think it is legitimate to point
out, in reply to the view that the speeches in the early part
of Acts are late compositions, that there is nothing in them
which suggests that which is *distinctive* of Paul.   This is not
true of other parts of Acts.   E.g., the phrase " the Spirit of
Jesus " in Acts xvi. 7 is unique in the N.T., but is only a slight
modification of the expression, " the Spirit of Jesus Christ,"
which is not only peculiar to Paul, but is the product of his
distinctive doctrine of the Spirit.   Similarly in Acts xiii. 39,
we have the characteristic Pauline term " justification," and
in Acts xx. 28, the chief ministers of the local church are called
" bishops," a term which is otherwise applied to them only
by Paul or his imitators (Phil. i. 1, 1 Tim. iii. 2, Tit. i. 7).   No
Pauline influence of this kind can be alleged against the
earlier speeches.

imitation of the translation-Greek of the
Septuagint, and which can be traced in other
parts of the Lucan work. It can be shown to
be Aramaism, of a kind similar to that which
we recognize in the report of the sayings of
Jesus in the Gospels. There is therefore a high
degree of probability that the author was laying under contribution an Aramaic source or
sources, whether written or oral, and whether
the work of translation had already been done,
or whether he translated it for himself.[1]

---

[1] See Torrey, *Composition and Date of Acts*. De Zwaan,
in *The Beginnings of Christianity*, edited by Jackson and Lake,
Part I, vol. ii, has subjected Torrey's theory to searching
examination, and concludes that the evidence for Aramaism
is strong for Acts i. 1–v. 16, ix. 31–xi. 18, quite doubtful for
v. 17–ix. 30, xi. 19–xiv. 28, and somewhat less doubtful for
xv. 1–36. All the speeches which concern us here, with the
exception of v. 29–32, fall within those sections in which the
evidence for Aramaism is strong, and for myself I cannot resist
the conclusion that the material here presented existed in
some form in Aramaic before it was incorporated in our Greek
Acts. According to Torrey, there are some examples of mis-
translation which would be natural in one whose knowledge of
Aramaic had been acquired at Antioch, and who was not well
acquainted with the southern Aramaic of Palestine.

In short, there is good reason to suppose that the speeches attributed to Peter in the Acts are based upon material which proceeded from the Aramaic-speaking Church at Jerusalem, and was substantially earlier than the period at which the book was written.

We may begin with the speeches in Acts ii–iv. There are four in all. The first two (ii. 14–36, 38–39) are supposed to have been delivered by Peter to the multitude assembled on the Day of Pentecost, the third (iii. 12–26) to the people after the healing of a lame man, and the fourth (iv. 8–12) to the Sanhedrin after the arrest of the apostles. The second account of the arrest in v. 17–40 is probably a doublet from another source, and it does not betray the same traces of Aramaism. The speech said to have been delivered on this occasion (v. 29–32) does no more than recapitulate briefly the substance of the previous speeches. The speech of Peter to Cornelius in ch. x. 34–43, is akin to the earlier speeches, but has some special features, and in it the evidence for an Aramaic original is at its strongest.

We may with some confidence take these speeches to represent, not indeed what Peter said upon this or that occasion, but the *kerygma* of the Church at Jerusalem at an early period.

The first four speeches of Peter cover substantially the same ground. The phraseology and the order of presentation vary slightly, but there is no essential advance from one to another. They supplement one another, and taken together they afford a comprehensive view of the content of the early *kerygma*. This may be summarized as follows :

First, the age of fulfilment has dawned. " This is that which was spoken by the prophet " (Acts ii. 16). " The things which God foreshewed by the mouth of all the prophets, He thus fulfilled " (iii. 18). " All the prophets from Samuel and his successors told of these days " (iii. 24). It was a standing principle of Rabbinic exegesis of the Old Testament that what the prophets predicted had reference to the " days of the Messiah," that is to say, to the expected time when God, after long centuries of waiting, should visit His people with judgment and blessing, bringing to a climax His dealings with them in history. The apostles, then, declare that the Messianic age has dawned.

Secondly, this has taken place through the ministry, death, and resurrection of Jesus, of which a brief account is given, with proof from the Scriptures that all took place through " the determinate counsel and fore-knowledge of God " : (*a*) His Davidic descent. " David, being a prophet, and knowing that God had sworn to set one of the fruit of his loins upon his throne, fore-saw (Christ)," who is therefore proclaimed, by implication, to have been born " of the seed of David " (ii. 30–31, citing Ps. cxxxii. 11). (*b*) His ministry. " Jesus of Nazareth, a man divinely accredited to you by works of power, prodigies, and signs which God did through Him among you " (Acts ii. 22).

" Moses said, The Lord your God will raise up a prophet like me ; him you must hear in everything that he may say to you " (Acts iii. 22, apparently regarded as fulfilled in the preaching and teaching of Jesus). (*c*) His death. " He was delivered up by the determinate counsel and foreknowledge of God, and you, by the agency of men without the law, killed Him by crucifixion " (ii. 23). " You caused Him to be arrested, and denied Him before Pilate, when he had decided to acquit Him. You denied the Holy and Righteous One, and asked for a murderer to be granted to you, while you killed the Prince of Life " (iii. 13–14). (*d*) His resurrection. " God raised Him up, having loosed the pangs of death, because it was not possible for Him to be held by it. For David says with reference to Him, ' Thou wilt not leave my soul in Hades, nor give Thy Holy One to see corruption ' " (ii. 24–31). " God raised Him from the dead, whereof we are witnesses " (iii. 15). " Jesus of Nazareth, whom you crucified, whom God raised from the dead " (iv. 10).

Thirdly, by virtue of the resurrection, Jesus has been exalted at the right hand of God, as Messianic head of the new Israel. "Being exalted at the right hand of God " (according to Ps. cx. 1). . . . " God has made Him Lord and Christ " (ii. 33–36). " The God of our fathers has glorified His Servant Jesus " (iii. 13). " He is the Stone which was rejected by you builders, and has become the top of the corner " (iv. 11, citing Ps. cxviii. 22). Cf. " God exalted Him at

His right hand, as Prince and Saviour "
(v. 31).

Fourthly, the Holy Spirit in the Church is
the sign of Christ's present power and glory.
" Being exalted at the right hand of God, and
having received the promise of the Holy
Spirit from the Father, He poured out this
which you see and hear " (Acts ii. 33). This
is documented from Joel ii. 28–32 (Acts ii.
17–21). Cf. " We are witnesses of these
things, and so is the Holy Spirit which God
has given to those who obey Him " (v. 32).

Fifthly, the Messianic Age will shortly
reach its consummation in the return of
Christ. " That He may send the Messiah
appointed beforehand for you, Jesus, whom
heaven must receive until the times of the
restoration of all things, of which God spoke

through the mouth of His prophets from of old " (iii. 21). This is the only passage in Acts i–iv which speaks of the second advent of Christ. In Acts x this part of the *kerygma* is presented in these terms : " This is He who is appointed by God as Judge of living and dead " (x. 42). There is no other explicit reference to Christ as Judge in these speeches.

Finally, the *kerygma* always closes with an appeal for repentance, the offer of forgiveness and of the Holy Spirit, and the promise of " salvation," that is, of " the life of the Age to Come," to those who enter the elect community. " Repent and be baptized, each of you, upon the name of Jesus Christ for the remission of your sins, and you will receive the gift of the Holy Spirit. For the promise is for you and your children, and for all those far off, whom the Lord your God may call " (Acts ii. 38–39, referring to Joel ii. 32, Is. lvii. 19).   " Repent therefore and be converted for the blotting out of your sins. . . . You are the sons of the prophets and of the covenant which God made with your fathers, saying to Abraham, ' And in thy seed shall all families of the earth be blessed.'   For you in the first place God raised up His Servant Jesus and sent Him to bless you by turning each of you away from your sins " (Acts iii. 19, 25–26, citing Gen. xii. 3).   " In no other is there salvation, for there is no other name under heaven given among men by which you must be saved " (Acts iv. 12).   Cf. " God exalted Him at His right hand as Prince and Saviour, to give repentance to Israel, and remission of sins" (Acts v. 31); "To Him all the prophets bear witness, that everyone who believes in Him shall receive remission of sins through His name " (Acts x. 43).

We may take it that this is what the author of Acts meant by " preaching the Kingdom of God." It is very significant that it follows the lines of the summary of the preaching of Jesus as given in Mark i. 14–15 : " Jesus came into Galilee preaching the Gospel of God, and saying, ' The time is fulfilled, and the Kingdom of God has drawn near : repent and believe the Gospel.' " This summary provides the framework within which the Jerusalem *kerygma* is set.

The first clause, " The time is fulfilled," is expanded in the reference to prophecy and its

fulfilment.   The second clause, " The Kingdom of God has drawn near," is expanded in
the account of the ministry and death of Jesus,
His resurrection and exaltation, all conceived
as an eschatological process.   The third
clause, " Repent and believe the Gospel,"
reappears in the appeal for repentance and
the offer of forgiveness with which the
apostolic *kerygma* closes.   Whether we say
that the apostolic preaching was modelled
on that of Jesus, or that the evangelist formu-
lated his summary of the preaching of
Jesus on the model of that of the primitive
Church, at any rate the two are identical in
purport.   The Kingdom of God is conceived as coming in the events of the life,
death, and resurrection of Jesus, and to
proclaim these facts, in their proper setting,

is to preach the Gospel of the Kingdom of God.

It is clear, then, that we have here, as in the preaching which we found to lie behind the Pauline epistles, a proclamation of the death and resurrection of Jesus Christ, in an eschatological setting from which those facts derive their saving significance. We may proceed to compare the two versions of the *kerygma*, in Paul and in the Acts respectively.

There are three points in the Pauline *kerygma* which do not directly appear in the Jerusalem *kerygma* of Acts :

(i) Jesus is not there called " Son of God." His titles are taken rather from the prophecies of Deutero-Isaiah. He is the holy and righteous " Servant " of God. It is noteworthy that the first person who is

said in Acts to have " preached Jesus, that
He is the Son of God," is Paul himself
(ix. 20). It may be that this represents an
actual difference of terminology. Yet the
idea that Jesus, as Messiah, is Son of God is
deeply embedded in the Synoptic Gospels,
whose sources were in all probability not
subject to Pauline influence ; and the Christological formula in Rom. i. 1–4 is, as we have
seen, probably not Pauline in origin. The
phrase " Son of God with power " there
carries much the same ideas as the phrase
" Lord and Christ " in the Jerusalem
kerygma, for its significance is Messianic
rather than properly theological.

(ii) The Jerusalem *kerygma* does not assert
that Christ died *for our sins*. The result of
the life, death, and resurrection of Christ is

the forgiveness of sins, but this forgiveness is not specifically connected with His death. Since, however, Paul includes this statement in that which he " received," we may hesitate to ascribe to him the origin of the idea. Since the Jerusalem *kerygma* applies to Christ the Isaianic title of " Servant," the way was at least open to interpret His death on the lines of Isaiah liii. Acts viii. 32–35 may suggest the possibility that this step was taken explicitly by the school of Stephen and Philip, with which Paul appears to have been in touch.

(iii) The Jerusalem *kerygma* does not assert that the exalted Christ intercedes for us. It may be that in Rom. viii. 34 Paul has inserted this on his own account into the apostolic formula. But, on the other hand,

4

the idea occurs also in Hebrews vii. 25 and seems to be implied in Matt. x. 32, so that it may not be of Pauline origin. It is perhaps, in effect, another way of saying that forgiveness is offered " in His name."

For the rest, all the points of the Pauline preaching reappear : the Davidic descent of Jesus, guaranteeing His qualification for Messiahship ; His death according to the Scriptures ; His resurrection according to the Scriptures ; His consequent exaltation to the right hand of God as Lord and Christ ; His deliverance of men from sin into new life ; and His return to consummate the new Age. This coincidence between the apostolic preaching as attested by the speeches in Acts, and as attested by Paul, enables us to carry back its essential elements to a date far earlier than a critical analysis of Acts by itself could justify ; for, as we have seen, Paul must have received the tradition very soon after the death of Jesus.

With this in view, we may usefully draw attention to other points in the Jerusalem *kerygma* which reappear in the epistles of Paul, though he does not explicitly include them in his " Gospel."

The *kerygma* in Acts lays emphasis upon the Holy Spirit in the Church as the sign that the new age of fulfilment has begun. The idea of the Spirit in the Church is very prominent in the Pauline epistles. We are now justified in concluding that this was no innovation of his, but represents a part of the tradition he had received. It is to be observed that in Gal. iii. 2 Paul appeals to

the evidence of the Spirit in the Church as a
datum from which he may argue regarding
the nature and conditions of salvation in
Christ, and on this basis he develops his
doctrine of the Spirit as the " earnest," or
first instalment, of the consummated life of
the Age to Come (2 Cor. i. 22, v. 5 ; Eph. i.
13-14).   This is true to the implications of
the *kerygma* as we have it in Acts.

Again, the " calling " and " election " of
the Church as the " Israel of God " can now
be seen to be no peculiarity of Pauline teaching.   It is implied in such passages of the
kerygma as Acts iii. 25–26, ii. 39.

There is, indeed, very little in the Jerusalem *kerygma* which does not appear, substantially, in Paul.   But there is one important element which at first sight at least

is absent from his preaching, so far as we can recover it from the epistles, namely, the explicit reference to the ministry of Jesus, His miracles (Acts ii. 22) and teaching (Acts iii. 22). Such references are only slight in the first four speeches of Peter, to which we have so far given most attention. But the case is different in the speech attributed to Peter in Acts x. 34-43. The principal elements of the *kerygma* can be traced in this speech—the fulfilment of prophecy, the death and resurrection of Christ, His second advent, and the offer of forgiveness. But all is given with extreme brevity, except the section dealing with the historical facts concerning Jesus. These are here treated in fairly full outline.

The Greek of x. 35-38 is notoriously rough

and ungrammatical, and indeed scarcely translatable, though the general meaning is clear. This is strange in so excellent a Greek writer as the author of Acts. In some MSS. it has been improved. But Dr. Torrey has shown that if the text in its more difficult form (which on general principles of textual criticism is likely to be more original) be translated word for word into Aramaic, it becomes both grammatical and perspicuous. The case, therefore, for regarding the passage as a translation is strong. I shall here follow Dr. Torrey, and give the passage after his restored Aramaic, being convinced that by doing so we shall come nearer to the original form.

" As for the word which He, the Lord of all, sent to the children of Israel, preaching the Gospel of peace through Jesus the Messiah, you know the thing (literally, ' the word ') that happened through all Judæa, beginning from Galilee after the baptism which John preached ; that God anointed Jesus of Nazareth with Holy Spirit and power ; and He went about doing good and healing all who were oppressed by the devil, because God was with Him.   And we are witnesses of all that He did in the country of the Jews and Jerusalem.   Him they killed by hanging Him upon a tree.   God raised Him up on the third day, and permitted Him to be manifest, not to all the people, but to witnesses chosen beforehand by God, namely to us, who ate and drank with Him after He rose from the dead."

It is to be observed that the first clause,

" the word which He sent to the children of Israel, preaching the Gospel of peace through Jesus Christ," which forms a sort of heading to the whole, is a virtual equivalent of the term " *kerygma* " or " Gospel." The passage is therefore offered explicitly as a form of apostolic preaching. It is represented as being delivered by Peter to a Gentile audience. It is quite intelligible in the situation presupposed that some account of the ministry of Jesus should have been called for when the Gospel was taken to people who could not be acquainted, as the Jews of Judæa were, with the main facts. We may perhaps take it that the speech before Cornelius represents the form of *kerygma* used by the primitive Church in its earliest approaches to a wider public.

In the preaching attested by Paul, although it was similarly addressed to the wider public, there does not seem to be any such comprehensive summary of the facts of the ministry of Jesus, as distinct from the facts of His death and resurrection. It would, however, be rash to argue from silence that Paul completely ignored the life of Jesus in his preaching; for, as we have seen, that preaching is represented only fragmentarily, and as it were accidentally, in the epistles. That he was aware of the historical life of Jesus, and cited His sayings as authoritative, need not be shown over again. It may be, for all we know, that the brief recital of historical facts in 1 Cor. xv. 1 *sqq.* is only the conclusion of a general summary which may have included some reference to the ministry.   But this remains uncertain.

According to Acts, Paul did preach in terms closely similar to those of the Petrine *kerygma* of Acts x.   The speech said to have been delivered by Paul at Pisidian Antioch (Acts xiii. 16–41) is too long to be quoted here in full, but the gist of it is as follows :

God brought Israel out of Egypt, and gave them David for their king.   Of the seed of David Jesus has come as Saviour. He was heralded by John the Baptist.   His disciples followed Him from Galilee to Jerusalem.   There He was brought to trial by the rulers of the Jews before Pilate, who reluctantly condemned Him.   He died according to the Scriptures, and was buried. God raised Him from the dead, according to the Scriptures, and He was seen by witnesses. Through Him forgiveness and justification are offered.   Therefore take heed.

This is obviously of the same stuff as the *kerygma* in the early chapters of Acts.   It may be compared on the one hand with the speeches in Acts ii–iv, and on the other hand with the speech in Acts x.   It is a mixture of the two types.   In particular, its historical *data* are fuller than those of Acts ii–iv, but less full than those of Acts x, containing no allusions to the baptism of Jesus or His miracles in Galilee.   There is nothing specifically Pauline in it, except the term " justification."   On the other hand, the

general scheme, and the emphasis, correspond with what we have found in the
epistles, and there is little or nothing in it
which could not be documented out of the
epistles, except the historical details in the
introductory passage (xiii. 16–22) and the
specific allusions to episodes in the Gospel
story, and in particular to the ministry of
John the Baptist (the fullest account in the
New Testament outside the Gospels) and
the trial before Pilate.

That these two episodes did not fall
wholly outside the range of Paul's interest
might perhaps be argued on the following
grounds.

(i) Paul refers in his epistles to Apollos
as one whom he would regard as a fellow-
worker, though others set him up as a rival.

Now, according to Acts, Apollos had been a follower of John the Baptist. Paul therefore must have had occasion to relate the work of the Baptist to the Christian faith.

(ii) In 1 Tim. vi. 13 we have an allusion to Christ's "confession before Pontius Pilate." Although we should probably not accept 1 Timothy as an authentic Pauline letter, yet it no doubt represents the standpoint of the Pauline circle, and the allusion to Pilate may have been derived from Paul's preaching.

These observations are far from proving that Paul would have included such references to John the Baptist and to the trial before Pilate in his preaching, but they show that it is not impossible that he may have done so, in spite of the silence of his epistles. In any case, if we recall the close general similarity of the *kerygma* as derived from the Pauline epistles to the *kerygma* as derived from Acts, as well as Paul's emphatic assertion of the identity of his Gospel with the general Christian tradition, we shall not find it altogether incredible that the speech at Pisidian Antioch may represent in a general way one form of Paul's preaching, that form, perhaps, which he adopted in synagogues when he had the opportunity of speaking there. If that is so, then we must say that he, like other early Christian preachers, gave a place in his preaching to some kind of recital of the facts of the life and ministry of Jesus.

If he did not do so, then we must say that in this respect he departed from the common model of apostolic preaching. For it seems clear that within the general scheme of the *kerygma* was included some reference, however brief, to the historical facts of the life of Jesus. These facts fall within the eschatological setting of the whole, no less than the facts of His death and resurrection. They are themselves eschatological events, in the sense that they form part of the process by which God's purpose reaches fulfilment and His Kingdom comes.

A comparison, then, of the Pauline epistles with the speeches in Acts leads to a fairly clear and certain outline sketch of the preaching of the apostles. That it is primitive in the strictest sense does not necessarily follow. In one respect it appears that even within a very few years the perspective of the *kerygma* must have altered, namely, in respect of the relation conceived to exist between the death, resurrection, and exaltation of Christ on the one hand, and His second advent on the other.

It is remarkable that the expectation of a very early advent persisted so long in the Church. Even in so late a writing as the First Epistle of John (ii. 18) the belief is expressed that this is " the last hour." The appendix to the Fourth Gospel is evidence that so long as one survivor of the generation of the apostles remained, the Church clung to the belief that during his lifetime the Lord would come (John xxi. 20–23). The expectation of a *speedy* advent must have had extraordinarily deep roots in Christian belief.

When Paul wrote to the Thessalonians in A.D. 50 he clearly expected it very soon indeed, and the qualifications he introduces in 2 Thessalonians seem to have been of the nature of an afterthought of which he had said nothing in his preaching. It is clearly the result of reflection upon the fact that the advent had been unexpectedly delayed. His first preaching had left the Thessalonians completely surprised and bewildered when certain of their fellows died and yet the Lord had not come. If Paul preached in these terms at least twenty years after the beginning of the Church, we may suppose that the announcement of a very speedy advent was even more emphatic at an earlier date.

In the Jerusalem *kerygma* there is an

5

equal sense of immediacy. It seems to be implied in Acts iii. 19–20 that the repentance of Israel in response to the appeal of the apostles will immediately be followed by " times of refreshing," by the return of Christ, and by the " restoration of all things." And here again we may recall, that early as the source may be, the passage in question was not written down until much water had flowed under the bridge.

What was the attitude of the apostles at the beginning ? We must remember that the early Church handed down as a saying of the Lord, " The Kingdom of God has come upon you " (Matt. xii. 28, Luke xi. 20). This means that the great divine event, the *eschaton*, has already entered history. In agreement with this, the preaching both of

Paul and of the Jerusalem Church affirms that the decisive thing has *already* happened. The prophecies are fulfilled ; God has shown His " mighty works " ; the Messiah has come ; He has been exalted to the right hand of God ; He has given the Spirit which according to the prophets should come " in the last days." Thus all that remains is the completion of that which is already in being. It is not to introduce a new order of things that the Lord will come ; it is only to finish His work. The Church believed that the Lord had said, " You will see the Son of Man seated on the right hand of the Power and coming with the clouds of heaven " (Mark xiv. 62). One part of the vision was fulfilled : by the eye of faith they already saw Him on the right hand of God.

Why should the conclusion of the vision delay ?

The more we try to penetrate in imagination to the state of mind of the first Christians in the earliest days, the more are we driven to think of resurrection, exaltation, and second advent as being, in their belief, inseparable parts of a single divine event. It was not an *early* advent that they proclaimed, but an *immediate* advent. They proclaimed it not so much as a future event for which men should prepare by repentance, but rather as the impending corroboration of a present fact : the new age is already here, and because it is here men should repent. The proof that it was here was found in the actual presence of the Spirit, that is, of the supernatural in the experience of men. It was in a supernatural world that the apostles felt themselves to be living; a world therefore in which it was natural that any day the Lord might be seen upon the clouds of heaven. That was what their Lord had meant, they thought, by saying, " The Kingdom of God has come upon you," while He also bade them pray, " Thy Kingdom come."

It is to be observed that the apostolic preaching as recorded in Acts does not (contrary to a commonly held opinion) lay the greatest stress upon the expectation of a second advent of the Lord. It is only in Acts iii. 20–21 that this expectation is explicitly and fully set forth, and only in Acts x. 42 that Christ is described as Judge of quick and dead. The speeches of Acts ii, iv, and v, as well as the professedly Pauline speech of Acts xiii, contain no explicit reference to it. That it is implied in the whole *kerygma* is true, but the emphasis does not lie there. The main burden of the *kerygma* is that the unprecedented has happened: God has visited and redeemed His people.

This conviction persists as fundamental to Christian belief through all changes in the whole of the New Testament. Paul speaks of the " new creation " which has taken place when a man is " in Christ " (2 Cor. v. 16). He says that God has already " rescued us out of the domain of darkness and transferred us into the kingdom of the Son of His love " (Col. i. 13). The Epistle to the Hebrews says that Christians have "tasted the powers of the Age to Come" (vi. 6). 1 Peter says that Christians have been "born again" (i. 3, 23). So does the Fourth Gospel (iii. 3). It needs only a slight acquaintance with the traditional Jewish eschatology to recognize that these writers are all using language which implies that the *eschaton*, the final and decisive act of God, has already entered human experience.

This is surely primitive. In the earliest days it was possible to hold this conviction in the indivisible unity of an experience which included also the expectation of an immediate overt confirmation of its truth. The great act of God had already passed through the stages of the sending of the Messiah, His miraculous works and authoritative teaching, His death (according to the determinate counsel and foreknowledge of God), His resurrection, and His exaltation to the right hand of God. It now trembled upon the verge of its conclusion in His second advent.

As time went on, the indivisible unity of experience which lay behind the preaching of the apostles was broken. The Lord did not come on the clouds. For all their conviction of living in an age of miracle, the apostles found themselves living in a world which went on its course, outside the limits of the Christian community, much as it had always done. The tremendous crisis in which they had felt themselves to be living passed, without reaching its expected issue. The second advent of the Lord, which had seemed to be impending as the completion of that which they had already " seen and heard," came to appear as a second crisis yet in the future. So soon as only a few years had passed, say three or four, this division in the originally indivisible experience must have insensibly taken place in their minds, for they were intercalary years, so to speak, not provided for in their first calendar of the divine purpose. The consequent demand for readjustment was a principal cause of the development of early Christian thought.

II

The Gospels

The Gospels

THE PREACHING OF the primitive Church had, as we have seen, an eschatological setting. Its terms were borrowed from the traditional eschatology of Judaism. But it differed from all earlier prophecy and apocalypse in declaring that the eschatological process was already in being. The Kingdom of God had made its appearance with the coming of the Messiah ; His works of power and His "new teaching with authority" had provided evidence of the presence of God among men ; His death " according to the determinate counsel and foreknowledge of God " had marked the end of the old order, and His resurrection and exaltation had definitely inaugurated the new age, characterized, as the prophets had foretold, by the outpouring of the Holy Spirit upon the people of God. It remained only for the new order to be consummated by the return of Christ in glory to judge the quick and the dead and to save His own from the wrath to come. The whole was conceived as a continuous, divinely directed process, in which past, present, and future alike had eschatological significance. In the recent past lay the ministry, death, and resurrection of Jesus Christ; the experience of the present attested His power in the Church through the Spirit; the near future would bring the final revelation of the meaning of the whole.

When the unexpected delay in the consummation broke up the continuity of the
eschatological process, some readjustment
of outlook was called for.   The lines along
which it took place depended upon the relative emphasis placed upon the past, the
present, or the future aspect of the primitive
Gospel.

For some minds, the most intense emotion
gathered about the thought of the expected
advent of the Lord.   The finished work of
Christ, and its results in the present experience of the Church, existed in the mind as a
permanent background of faith, producing
that atmosphere of " joy and simplicity of
heart " which the author of Acts (ii. 46)
notes as characteristic of the early days.
But all this was, after all, in some sort pro-

visional and incomplete; it was preparatory to the glory yet to be revealed when the Lord should return on the clouds of heaven. As the revelation still delayed, the believers were driven to conclude that they had been mistaken in thinking that the Lord would return immediately, but a more attentive study of His teaching, and observation of the signs of the times, they thought, would enable them to divine the time of His coming, as well as the reason for its delay. The Church therefore proceeded to reconstruct on a modified plan the traditional scheme of Jewish eschatology which had been broken up by the declaration that the Kingdom of God had already come. Materials for such a reconstruction were present in profusion in the apocalyptic literature. The recon-

structed eschatology of the Church therefore
drew heavily on Jewish sources.

The earliest document of this tendency is
to be found in 2 Thessalonians. The
eschatological passage in the first chapter of
that epistle (7–10), which most critics have
noted as being in style unlike that of Paul,
is best understood as a virtual quotation of
some current apocalypse, whether Jewish or
Jewish-Christian. There is nothing distinctively Christian either in its contents or
in its general tone, apart from the fact that
the figure of the Messiah is identified with
Jesus. In the second chapter (3–10) we
have a peculiar doctrine which may have
been contained in the same apocalypse. It
is clearly an adaptation of the ancient myth
of Anti-Christ or Beliar, who now appears in
6

the guise of the " Man of Sin." Clearly the motive underlying it is the problem, Why has the Lord not yet come ? The answer is, that His coming must be preceded, as ancient apocalypses had foretold, by the outbreak of final anarchy, and this outbreak is delayed by the " restraining power," which is probably to be understood as the power of the Roman Empire. Nevertheless, " the Mystery of Iniquity " is already at work. Shortly, the restraining power will be removed. The Man of Sin will appear, claiming divine honours, and will commit a horrible sacrilege in the Temple of God. That will be the signal for the immediate coming of the Lord to judgment.

It may well be that those critics are right who suggest that the model who sat for this portrait of the Man of Sin was the mad Emperor Caligula, whose attempt to set up his image in the Temple had deeply affronted Jewish sentiment, recalling, as it did, the sacrilege of Antiochus Epiphanes, which Daniel had described as " the abomination of desolation." That attempt failed, but it showed that the Mystery of Iniquity was already at work, and a second such attempt would precipitate the final crisis. The point to be observed is that an explanation is being offered of the delay of the Lord's advent, along with an indication of the infallible signs which will precede that event.

A similar motive is to be discerned in the " Little Apocalypse " of Mark xiii. It is unnecessary to demonstrate over again that this apocalypse, though it contains embedded in it sayings belonging to the primitive tradition of the teaching of Jesus, is inconsistent with the purport of His teaching as a whole, and presupposes knowledge of events after His death. The writer has in view the disturbed political situation of the late fifties of early sixties, the " wars and rumours of wars " upon the eastern frontier of the Empire, the famines and earthquake shocks recorded under Claudius and Nero, and the growing isolation and unpopularity of the Christian Church ; but he is concerned to assure his readers that " the end is not yet." First the horrible sacrilege must take place —" the abomination of desolation standing where he ought not," and *then* will come the final tribulation, the collapse of the physical universe and the appearance of the Son of Man upon the clouds of heaven.

These two documents illustrate clearly the character of the reconstructed eschatology of the early Church. It has undoubtedly influenced the tradition of the teaching of Jesus in the Synoptic Gospels.[1] The First Gospel is most deeply affected by it, but none of the three is entirely exempt. This is natural, since the tradition had undergone considerable development before it was embodied in our canonical Gospels, and during this time it had been exposed to the influence of what we may call the " futurist eschatology," as distinct from the " realized eschatology " which gives its character to the

---

[1] See my book, *The Parables of the Kingdom* (Nisbet, 1935), chs. iv–vi.

earliest preaching, as well as to the earliest tradition of the teaching of Jesus.

This "futurist" tendency reaches its climax, within the New Testament, in the Revelation of John. As a piece of apocalyptic literature it takes its place naturally in the series which begins with the Book of Daniel, and includes such works as the Book of Enoch, the Assumption of Moses, the Apocalypse of Baruch, and 2 Esdras. The whole apparatus of Jewish apocalyptic is here adapted to Christian use. In cryptic imagery the writer refers to current and immediately impending events—the political conflicts of the time, the Parthian menace, the fear of a return of Nero, the growth of Cæsar-worship, and the intensification of persecution—and interprets these as the infallible signs of the approaching advent of the Lord. The whole emphasis falls upon that which is to come.

The other elements in the *kerygma* are indeed present as a background. The death and resurrection of the Lord are presupposed as the condition of His ultimate triumph, and He is seen in vision walking in the midst of the golden candlesticks which are the churches. But all this is subordinated to the intense expectation of glory yet to come, which absorbs the writer's real interest. And if we review the book as a whole, we must judge that this excessive emphasis on the future has the effect of relegating to a secondary place just those elements in the original Gospel which are most distinctive of Christianity—the faith that in the finished work of Christ God has already acted for the salvation of man, and the blessed sense of living in the divine presence here and now.

Under the influence of this revived Jewish eschatology, Christianity was in danger of falling back into the position of the earlier apocalyptists. Minds dominated by the fantastic visions of the Revelation of John might easily lose the sense that all had been made new by the coming of Christ, and that in the communion of His people the life of the Age to Come was a present possession, through the Spirit which He had given. They would then be in no better case than, say, the authors of the apocalypses of Baruch and Ezra, for whom the present had no divine significance, but all the energy of faith was absorbed in picturing that which should come to pass. That would amount to a denial of the substance of the Gospel.

The effects of this relapse into a pre-Christian eschatology are evident in the tone and temper of the Revelation itself. With all the magnificence of its imagery and the splendour of its visions of the majesty of God and the world to come, we are bound to judge that in its conception of the character of God and His attitude to man the book falls below the level, not only of the teaching of Jesus, but of the best parts of the Old Testament. Our Lord's proclamation of the Kingdom of God was associated with a new conception of the infinite loving-kindness of the heavenly Father. It was " a new teaching, with authority." Where shall we find its echoes in the Revelation of

John ?   At most, in a verse or two here and there.   The God of the Apocalypse can hardly be recognized as the Father of our Lord Jesus Christ, nor has the fierce Messiah, whose warriors ride in blood up to their horses' bridles, many traits that could recall Him of whom the primitive *kerygma* proclaimed that He went about doing good and healing all who were oppressed by the devil, because God was with Him.

This line of development led into a blind alley.   In the second century its stream of thought ran out into the barren sands of millenarianism, which in the end was disavowed by the Church.   Attempts to revive it in later periods have always had something artificial and fanatical about them.   When their authors claim to be returning to primitive Christianity, they ignore the fact that it is impossible ever to revive the belief that the Lord would in literal truth arrive to judgment upon the clouds of heaven during the thirties of the first century. He did not do so. To work up a fantastic expectation that He will arrive in the thirties of the twentieth century is not primitive Christianity, whatever it may be.

The possibility of eschatological fanaticism was no doubt present in the outlook of the primitive Church, but it was restrained by the essential character of the Gospel as apprehended in experience. The exposure of the illusion which fixed an early date for the Lord's advent, while it threw some minds back into the unwholesome ferment of apocalyptic speculation, gave to finer minds the occasion for grasping more firmly the substantive truths of the Gospel, and finding for them a more adequate expression.

To return to the primitive *kerygma*, we recall that in it the expectation of the Lord's return was held in close association with a definite valuation of His ministry, death, and resurrection as constituting in themselves an eschatological process, that is, as a decisive manifestation of the mighty acts of God for the salvation of man. Eschatology is not itself the substance of the Gospel, but a form under which the absolute value of the Gospel facts is asserted. The second advent is not the supreme fact, to which all else is preparatory ; it is the impending verification of the Church's faith that the finished work of Christ has in itself absolute value.

Thus the authentic line of development, as the expectation of an immediate advent faded, led to a concentration of attention upon the historical facts of the ministry, death, and resurrection of Jesus, exhibited in an eschatological setting which made clear their absolute and final quality as saving facts.

This line of development can be traced in the Pauline and other epistles.

We have already seen that Paul's preaching was centred in the proclamation of the facts of the death and resurrection of Christ. His interpretation of these facts starts from the application to them of eschatological categories. Thus he says that in the death of Christ God manifested His righteousness [1]

[1] Rom. iii. 21-26.

and condemned sin in the flesh.[1] The manifestation of righteousness and the condemnation of sin are functions of the Last Judgment. Again, he says that in the Cross God triumphed over principalities and powers.[2] The overthrow of the " kingdom of the enemy " is in eschatological tradition the coming of the Kingdom of God, that is, the ultimate divine event. Similarly, the resurrection of Christ is for Paul the first stage of that transfiguration of human nature into a heavenly condition which the apocalypses predicted. He is the " first-fruits of them that sleep," [3] the " first-born from the dead," [4] and in union with Him Christians have already experienced the

[1] Rom. viii. 3.
[2] Col. ii. 15.
[3] 1 Cor. xv. 20.
[4] Col. i. 18.

" new creation," and are " being transfigured from glory to glory." [1]   Thus the death and resurrection of Christ are interpreted as the divinely ordained crisis in history through which old things passed away and the new order came into being.

It is in this light that we must understand all that Paul says about redemption, justification, and the end of the Law.   The " redemption " of Israel out of Egyptian slavery had already become for the prophets a foreshadowing of the ultimate " redemption " of the people of God from all the evil of this present age.[2]   It is this ultimate (eschatological) " redemption " that Paul sees to have been accomplished through the death

[1] 2 Cor. v. 16, Gal. vi. 15, 2 Cor. iii. 18.
[2] See Exod. xv. 13, Deut. vii. 8, Is. i. 27, Jer. xxxi. 11, Is. li. 11, etc.

and resurrection of Christ. Again, the very idea of " justification " implies a judgment which has already taken place. The righteousness of God is already revealed, and it has taken the form, as the prophets had foreseen that it would, of the " justification " of His people. And nothing short of the appearance of the Age to Come could supersede the Law, which was the complete expression of the purpose of God for man in " this age." In dying to the Law, and rising into newness of life, Christ had made the decisive transition, on behalf of the whole people of God.

Finally, the philosophy of history expounded in Rom. ix–xi, and more allusively elsewhere, with its acute and convincing valuation of the stages of Hebrew and

Jewish history, implies a corresponding valuation of the events in which, for Paul, that history reached fulfilment, the death and resurrection of Jesus Christ. These events have the actuality which belongs to the historical process as such, and at the same time they possess the absolute significance which belongs to the *eschaton*, the ultimate fulfilment of the divine purpose in history.

In the First Epistle of Peter the reader is aware of an atmosphere which seems in some respects nearer to that of the primitive Church, as we divine it behind the early chapters of Acts, than anything else in the New Testament. That in general its thought follows the apostolic preaching is clear, and we could easily believe that in places its very

7

language is echoed. For this writer the
theme of all prophecy is " the sufferings of
Christ and the glory to follow " (i. 11).
His death, which took place " at the end of
the times," is the fulfilment of the eternal
counsel of God (i. 20). He died for sins,
rose again, ascended into heaven, and is on
the right hand of God, angels, principalities,
and powers being subject to Him (iii. 18–22).
In the light of our previous study, we shall
not be so ready as some critics have been
to put all this down to " Pauline influence."
It is a clear echo of the apostolic preaching
which lies behind Paul and the whole New
Testament.

But it is of particular interest to observe
that this writer does not dwell exclusively
on the bare fact that Christ died for our sins,

but attaches saving significance to His
character, and His behaviour on trial :
" He did no sin, neither was any guile found
in His mouth. When He was abused, He
did not retort with abuse. Under suffering
He uttered no threats, but committed Himself to Him who judges justly " (ii. 22–23).
It has often been pointed out that this description is partly modelled on Isaiah liii,
which describes the sufferings of the Servant
of the Lord ; but I venture to think that the
wrong inference has often been drawn from
this fact. It has been said that the writer is
not following any historical tradition of the
life of Jesus, but drawing freely from prophecy an ideal picture of the suffering
Messiah. This is to miss the point. For
this writer, as for other early Christian

thinkers, the important thing is the correspondence of prophecy with the facts. That Isaiah foretold such behaviour on the part of the Servant of the Lord is important just because Jesus did in fact so behave : " *this* is that which was spoken by the prophet." Here, therefore, not simply the fact that Jesus suffered and died, but the way in which His character was exhibited in His sufferings, is a part of the " eschatological " fulfilment. This goes beyond anything that is explicitly said by Paul, though it may be said to be implied in such passages as Rom. v. 19, xv. 3 ; Phil. ii. 8.

In the Epistle to the Hebrews eschatology has been reinterpreted in terms of a Platonic scheme. The " Age to Come " is identified with that order of eternal reality whose shadows or reflections form the world of phenomena. The death of Christ, therefore, which in the primitive preaching was the crisis of the eschatological process, is here His passage into the eternal order (ix. 12, 24). By dying He has " consecrated a new and living way through the veil " which separated human experience from the world of supreme reality (x. 20). The death of Christ, therefore, is the point at which history becomes fully real, exhibiting no longer mere shadows, but " the very image of realities " (x. 1). The eschatological valuation of the death of Christ thus receives a new interpretation, which gives the clue to this writer's doctrine of His eternal priesthood.

In the Pauline epistles, therefore, in 1 Peter, and in Hebrews, the primitive valuation of the death and resurrection of Christ as " eschatological " events is developed in striking ways.   But in none of these writings is there any sustained attempt to give an eschatological interpretation to the facts of the ministry of Jesus apart from His passion, death, and resurrection, even though all three writers are aware that His death was the final expression of a character and a moral purpose which displayed itself in His whole incarnate life.   Paul records that Jesus was born under the Law,[1] that for our sakes He became poor,[2] that He pleased not Himself,[3] that He humbled Himself,[4] and that He was obedient in all things to the will of God ; [5]

[1] Gal. iv. 4.
[2] 2 Cor. viii. 9.   The reference is to the Incarnation, but the expression would be frigid if it had not been known that Jesus was actually a poor man.
[3] Rom. xv. 3.
[4] Phil. ii. 8.
[5] Rom. v. 19, Phil. ii. 8.

and these facts he sees to be essential to the saving effect of His death. In 1 Peter, as we have seen, His innocence and humility under trial are part of His fulfilment of the divine purpose as declared in the prophets. In Hebrews, the sacrificial character of His death is described in the Psalmist's words, " Lo, I am come to do Thy will, O God " (x. 5–9) ; and for this writer His trials and temptations,[1] His discipline of suffering,[2] and His agony in prayer [3] are all factors in the act by which He consecrated the new and living way through the veil. But the fact remains that for all these writers the life of Jesus is rather the preparation for His death and resurrection than itself a part of the decisive eschatological event. None of

[1] Heb. ii. 18, iv. 15.   [2] ii. 10.   [3] v. 7.

them does full justice to the place which the recital of the facts of the ministry holds in some forms of the apostolic preaching.

For a more thoroughgoing valuation of the life of Jesus in eschatological terms we must turn to the Synoptic Gospels, and in the first instance to Mark.

I have elsewhere [1] tried to show that we can trace in the Gospel according to Mark a connecting thread running through much of the narrative, which has some similarity to the brief summary of the story of Jesus in Acts x and xiii, and may be regarded as an expanded form of what we may call the historical section of the *kerygma*.

Let us recall the general scheme of the *kerygma*. It begins by proclaiming that

[1] *Expository Times*, vol. xliii. no. 9, pp. 396 *sqq.*, "The Framework of the Gospel Narrative."

" this is that which was spoken by the prophets " ; the age of fulfilment has dawned, and Christ is its Lord ; it then proceeds to recall the historical facts, leading up to the resurrection and exaltation of Christ and the promise of His coming in glory ; and it ends with the call to repentance and the offer of forgiveness. Now, if the Gospel according to Mark may be regarded as based upon an expanded form of the middle, or historical, section, we must observe that this section is not, in Mark any more than in the *kerygma*, isolated from the general scheme. The theme of Mark's Gospel is not simply the succession of events which ended in the crucifixion of Jesus. It is the theme of the *kerygma* as a whole. This is indeed indicated as the evangelist's intention by the opening

phrase which gives the title of the work :
" The beginning of the Gospel of Jesus
Christ." Some patristic writers refer to the
Gospels as " memoirs," thereby placing
them in a well-defined class of Greek literature. But the earliest evangelist does not so
describe his work. He describes it as
" Gospel," and this word, as we have seen,
is a virtual equivalent for *kerygma*. Mark
therefore conceived himself as writing a form
of *kerygma*, and that his Gospel is in fact a
rendering of the apostolic preaching will
become clear from an analysis of the book
itself.

After the opening phrase, which I have
already quoted, the Gospel begins : " As it is
written in Isaiah the prophet." This recalls the first words of the *kerygma* according

to Acts ii : " This is that which was spoken by the prophet." The theme of fulfilment is at once in view. The prophecies cited here are those which speak of the immediate prelude to the Day of the Lord, and these Mark sees fulfilled in the appearance of John the Baptist, of whose ministry a brief account is given, just sufficient to introduce the significant words, " A stronger than I is coming after me.[1] I baptized with water, but He will baptize you with Holy Spirit." Once again we have an echo of the *kerygma* of Acts, which finds in the descent of the Spirit the sign of the new Age. John's proclamation is followed immediately by the

[1] According to Acts xiii. 25 this was actually included in some forms of the apostolic Preaching, though as it does not usually enter into such details, we may perhaps suspect some influence of the Gospels reflected back upon the *kerygma* out of which they developed.

Baptism of Jesus, accompanied by a vision of the Holy Spirit, and the divine voice which acclaims Him as the Son of God. We know from Acts x. 38 that this event was interpreted as the " anointing " of Jesus, by which He was designated Messiah, i.e. the Anointed, in fulfilment of the prophecy in Isa. lxi. 1.   So far, therefore, Mark serves as a commentary on the *kerygma*, and explains why in even the very brief summaries of it which we have in Acts x and xiii so much stress is laid on the part taken by John the Baptist.

Mark now relates how Jesus came into Galilee preaching the Kingdom of God, and his summary of this preaching would serve, as we have seen, equally well for a skeleton outline of the preaching of the primitive

Church: " The time is fulfilled, and the Kingdom of God has drawn near. Repent and believe the Gospel."

Down to this point we are reading the exordium of the book, which serves quite definitely to place the whole narrative within the framework of the *kerygma*. From this point detailed narrative begins, chiefly in the form of more or less detached episodes, loosely strung upon the thread of an outline whose form can be recognized in the comparatively colourless summaries which link the episodes together, until with the story of the Passion we enter upon a continuous and highly wrought dramatic narrative.

The Passion-narrative itself occupies a disproportionately large section of the Gospel, almost exactly one-fifth of the whole.

Not only so, but rather more than half the Gospel, from the middle of chapter viii, is dominated by the thought of the approaching Passion. From the first announcement, " The Son of Man must suffer," in viii. 31, onward, the shadow of the Cross falls upon the whole story. This corresponds to the emphasis of the apostolic preaching, both in its formulation in Acts, and in its development in Paul and Hebrews. The earliest Gospel is pre-eminently a Gospel of the Passion.

The story of the Passion, however, is prefaced, in chs. i–viii, as it is in Acts x, by an account of the ministry of Jesus in Galilee when He went about doing good and healing those who were oppressed by the devil. Here again Mark serves as commentary on the *kerygma*, for his apparently artless series of episodes from the Galilæan ministry builds up a cumulative impression of the decisive significance of the facts. The works of Jesus are works of divine power. With authority He commands the unclean spirits, and Satan's dominion is at an end; for no one could plunder the strong man's house if he had not first bound the strong man. Not only in His death, Mark means to say, but in His ministry, Jesus overcame the principalities and powers. As the prophets had declared that in the Age to Come the eyes of the blind should be opened and the ears of the deaf unstopped, so Jesus heals the blind and the deaf, and restores strength to the palsied and life to the dead. He teaches, again, with authority and not as the scribes.   He dispenses men from the obligations of the law and the tradition, and pronounces the forgiveness of sins.   By His sovereign will He calls men, even those who are without the law, and they rise and follow.   And to those who follow He says, " To you is given the mystery of the Kingdom of God."

This all leads up to the momentous question, " Who do you say that I am ? " and Peter's reply, " Thou art the Messiah," puts into words the conviction that the whole narrative has been intended to create in the mind of the reader.   The Messiah has appeared, and in Him the Kingdom of God has come.   The story takes on its eschatological significance.   So now the way is clear for the proclamation of Christ and Him crucified. " The Son of Man must suffer many things, and be rejected, and rise again." The theme of the rest of the Gospel is " the sufferings of Christ and the glory to follow," which, as the First Epistle of Peter says, is the theme of all prophecy.

Observe how subtly the story of the Passion is set within a frame of glory. The first announcement of suffering is followed immediately by the vision of the glory of Christ in the story of the Transfiguration. The Lord appears attended by the historic figures of Moses and Elijah. Then the cloud of the divine glory descends upon Him and a voice declares, " This is my beloved Son " ; and forthwith Moses and Elijah are seen no more ; the law and the prophets have vanished in the moment of

8

their fulfilment, and " they saw no one but Jesus alone." Then follows the fateful journey to Jerusalem, punctuated with renewed predictions of the sufferings that await Him there, and ending with the Messianic entry into the city and the cleansing of the Temple. We recall the words of prophecy, " The Lord whom ye seek shall suddenly come to His temple, but who may abide the day of His coming?" (Mal. iii. 1-2).

And so the stage is set for the description of the Passion itself, which is given in a tone of unrelieved tragedy, with none of those alleviating touches which the other evangelists have allowed themselves. In its grim realism it is almost overwhelming to read. But once again, the tragedy is framed in glory. In ch. xiii Mark has interrupted the narrative to insert the apocalyptic discourse to which I have already referred. Considered as an independent composition, which it appears originally to have been, the Little Apocalypse must be held to belong to a line of development which had no real future before it. But as incorporated in the Gospel of the Passion it acquires a different perspective. For it serves to assure the reader that the story of suffering and defeat to which it is the immediate prelude has for its other side that eternal weight of glory which Christ attained through His passion. The balance of the original *kerygma* is restored.

This, then, is the introduction of the Passion-story. It ends on a similar note. The darkness which was upon the face of the whole earth while Christ died broods over the narrative until His dying cry is stilled. And then—" The veil of the Temple was rent in two from top to bottom." This rending of the veil we have already met with. It is the veil that lay between men and the presence of God. Christ has now consecrated a new and living way through the veil : God is revealed, in His kingdom, power, and glory. Not Paul himself could have set forth more startlingly the divine paradox of the glory of the Cross. " And when the centurion saw that He so died, he said, ' Truly this man was the Son of God.' " As Peter's confession prepared the way for the story of the Passion, so the confession of the pagan soldier provides the final comment upon it.

Mark then proceeded, according to the formula of the *kerygma* in 1 Cor. xv, to record how Christ was buried, and rose again the third day according to the Scriptures. But unfortunately only a fragment of his resurrection narrative has survived; enough, however, to show what the climax of the Gospel was. The story of the saving facts is complete.

We see clearly, therefore, how fitly Mark's work is described not as " memoirs " of Jesus, but as " Gospel." Whether the other early attempts to " compose a narrative of the facts that were accomplished among us," to which Luke refers in his preface, had the same character, it is impossible to say. But in any case the scheme of Gospel-writing laid down by Mark became the model on which the other canonical Gospels were composed.

We discern, however, in Matthew and Luke a certain departure from the original perspective and emphasis of the *kerygma*. In both of them the narrative of the passion, death, and resurrection of Jesus occupies a smaller proportion of the whole : in Matthew roughly one-seventh, in Luke about one-sixth, as compared with one-fifth in Mark ; and in estimating these proportions we must remember that when Mark was complete, its resurrection-narrative was certainly a good deal longer.

In both Matthew and Luke, however, an element in the *kerygma* receives emphasis which is not prominent in Mark, that, namely, which declared that Christ was "born of the seed of David," and so

qualified for Messiahship according to prophecy. The genealogies which both supply
are intended as documentation of this fact,
and in Matthew the descent from David is
frequently mentioned. The nativity narratives, on the other hand, which are in formal
contradiction to the genealogies (since these
trace the Davidic descent of Jesus through
Joseph, though he was not, according to
the nativity narratives, His father) cannot be
derived from the *kerygma*.[1]

Matthew further emphasizes the theme of
" fulfilment " by his practice of systemati-
cally citing prophecies which he regards as
fulfilled in various episodes of the life of

[1] In *Theologische Blätter*, December 1935, pp. 289-297, Professor Karl Ludwig Schmidt suggests that the story of the
Virgin Birth was derived from a form of tradition handed
down in relative secrecy.   Whether or not that was so, it has
no direct connection with the *kerygma*, which was in its nature
a *public* proclamation.

Jesus. The connections which he suggests sometimes appear to the modern reader artificial, but in substance his view is conformable to the apostolic preaching. For the rest, there are two main tendencies to be discerned in the First Gospel.

On the one hand, it contains, in addition to the Marcan narrative, a large collection of sayings of Jesus, arranged so as to form a fairly systematic account of His teaching. It is presented as a new Law given by the Messianic King. In the apostolic preaching, as we have seen, there is only slight allusion to the work of Jesus as Teacher. The incorporation of this fresh material has the effect of modifying in some degree the character in which Christianity is presented. It is not so much a Gospel of " realized

eschatology," as a new and higher code of
ethics. This change was natural enough;
for when it became necessary to readjust the
Christian outlook to the indefinite postpone-
ment of the second advent and judgment,
the Church had to organize itself as a permanent society living the life of the redeemed
people of God in an unredeemed world.
Everything, therefore, in the tradition of the
teaching of Jesus which could afford guid-
ance for the conduct of the community in
this situation came to be of especial value.
Matthew is, in fact, no longer in the pure
sense a " Gospel." It combines *kerygma*
with *didaché*, and if we regard the book as a
whole, the element of *didaché* predominates.[1]

---

[1] It has always been recognized that the document known as
the *Didaché*, or *Teaching of the Twelve Apostles*, has a special
affinity with the didactic portions of the First Gospel.

On the other hand, Matthew compensates for this change of emphasis by a marked development of "futurist eschatology." The expectation of the second advent has a larger place in this Gospel than in any other. We might express the distinctively Matthæan view of the Gospel somewhat after this fashion ; Christ came in fulfilment of prophecy as Messiah ; but His Messianic activity at His first coming consisted chiefly in the exposition of the new and higher Law by which His people should live until His second coming.   This line of thought clearly had great influence in determining the form in which popular Christianity emerged in the second century.

In Luke the change is more subtle.   We may describe it as due to an increased interest in Jesus as a human wonder-worker, as the friend and lover of men, especially of those who were without the law, as the ideal for Christian conduct. All this is no more than is implied in the phrase of the *kerygma* which describes Him as " going about doing good, because God was with Him," and it affords a necessary and valuable supplement to the Marcan picture of the strong Son of God, and the Matthæan picture of the royal Law-giver. But again it represents a certain modification of the original perspective. It is in some measure a rationalized and humanitarian rendering of the Gospel, de-signed to appeal to the average man of feel-ing. The exceptional powers of sympathetic imagination and of literary expression pos-sessed by this evangelist make his work the most effective of all as a human and, so to speak, secular approach to the " Jesus of History," but it does not lie on the main classical line of development from the apostolic preaching.

For the sake of brevity and emphasis, I have perhaps exaggerated the differences between Mark and the other Synoptic Gospels. The Gospels of Matthew and Luke do, after all, fall well within the general scheme of the *kerygma*, though they subtly alter its perspective. It is, however, in the Fourth Gospel that we return to the main line of development which runs through Mark from the original apostolic preaching ; though here the eschatological framework has been transformed into something widely different. One of the points in which the criticism of the last century was most notably at fault was its assumption that the line ran from Mark through Matthew and Luke to John. In some important respects Matthew and Luke represent side-tracks from the main line. But I shall have to return to the Fourth Gospel in the last lecture.

It is surely clear that the fourfold Gospel taken as a whole is an expression of the original apostolic preaching. Of this the early Church was well aware. The Muratorian Canon, probably representing the work of Hippolytus, the dissenting Bishop of Rome about the end of the second century, justifies the presence of four separate Gospels in the Canon of the New Testament in these terms :

" Although various principles are taught in the several Gospel-books, this makes no difference to the faith of believers, since by one governing Spirit in them all, the facts are declared concerning the Nativity, the Passion, the Resurrection, His converse with the disciples, and His two advents, the first which was in humility of aspect, according to the power of His royal Father, and the glorious one which is yet to come."

Hippolytus means that the four Gospels embody the original apostolic preaching of the " saving facts," and are as such accepted as authoritative by the Church.

I have not here considered the question of the historical value of the Gospels as a record of facts. That question is aside from the

immediate purpose of these lectures.   But I
would observe that the latest developments
in Gospel criticism have somewhat shifted
the incidence of the problem of historicity.
We are not to think of the record in the
Gospels as the ultimate raw material, out of
which the Preaching was constructed.   The
kerygma is primary, and it acted as a preserva-
tive of the tradition which conveyed the
facts.   The nearer we are in the Gospels to
the stuff of the *kerygma*, the nearer we are to
the fountain-head of the tradition.   There
never existed a tradition formed by a dry
historical interest in the facts as facts.   From
the beginning the facts were preserved in
memory and tradition as elements in the
Gospel which the Church proclaimed.

This, no doubt, means that we cannot

expect to find in the Gospels (except by accident, as, for example, in Mark xiv. 51–52) bare matter of fact, unaffected by the interpretation borne by the facts in the *kerygma*.   But it also means that wherever the Gospels keep close to the matter and form of the *kerygma*, there we are in touch with a tradition coeval with the Church itself.   For, as we have seen, a comparison of Paul and Acts enables us to trace the essential elements in the apostolic Preaching to a very early date indeed.   The history of Jesus, even as history, was of decisive importance for the tradition, just because in the Preaching the life, death, and resurrection of Jesus were held to be the climax of all history, the coming of the Kingdom of God.   I believe that a sober and instructed criticism of the Gospels justifies the belief that in their central and dominant tradition they represent the testimony of those who stood nearest to the facts, and whose life and outlook had been moulded by them.

9

III

Paul and John

Paul and John

IN THE LAST lecture we traced one line of
development from the original apostolic
preaching; that, namely, which starting from
the eschatological valuation of facts of the
past, the life, death, and resurrection of
Jesus Christ, resulted in the production of
that distinctively Christian form of literature
known as Gospels.   We have now to turn
once more to the primitive *kerygma*, with
special attention to that part of it which
attributed an eschatological significance to
facts of the present.

We have seen that the apostolic Preaching
according to Acts ii included an appeal to

the presence and work of the Holy Spirit in the Church as evidence that the age of fulfilment had dawned, and that Jesus Christ was its Lord. " This is that which was spoken by the prophet. . . . I will pour out my Spirit upon all flesh. . . . He being exalted at the right hand of God, and having received the promise of the Holy Spirit from the Father, has poured out that which you see and hear " ; and it includes also an assurance that those who join the Christian community " receive the gift of the Holy Spirit."

It is true that in other forms of the *kerygma* in Acts there is no such explicit reference to the Spirit in the Church, except in v. 32, which belongs to what is probably a secondary doublet of the story given in iii–iv.

It is true also that Paul does not expressly
say that the gift of the Spirit was a part of
what he proclaimed as Gospel.   But in Acts
and epistles alike it is clear that the fact of
life in the Spirit is presupposed.   The primitive Church, in proclaiming its Gospel to the
world, offered its own fellowship and experience as the realization of the Gospel.   This
is of the essence of the matter.   In the
Christian experience as it was enjoyed in the
fellowship, the early believers were confident
that they were in possession of the supernatural blessings which the prophets had
foretold.

Quite naïvely, they were impressed
by the abnormal psychical phenomena—
faith-healing, second sight, "speaking
with tongues," and the like—which broke

out at Pentecost, and accompanied the extension of Christianity beyond the borders of Judæa. The reality of these phenomena there is not the slightest reason to doubt. Paul himself declares that his missionary work was accomplished " in the power of signs and wonders, in the power of Holy Spirit " (Rom. xv. 19), and he regards " works of power, gifts of healing, divers kinds of tongues " (1 Cor. xii. 28) as normal in the life of the Church. We have now sufficient records of similar phenomena at other times of religious " revival," not only within Christianity, to justify the view that they are usual accompaniments of religious emotion raised to a certain pitch of intensity.

But it is clear that behind them lay, as Paul saw, a new quality of life, with which this

intense emotion was associated.   The naïve
interest of the author of Acts in the miraculous should not prevent us from recognizing
that he is in fact describing a corporate life
which had this new quality.   One thing he
definitely sets forth as the result of life in the
Spirit, namely, the social unity created by it,
which expressed itself alike in a remarkably
intimate fellowship in worship and in the
sharing of needs and resources.[1]   For this
special type of social unity Paul found the
fitting expression : " the fellowship of the
Holy Spirit " (2 Cor. xiii. 13, Phil. ii. 1).
The phrase is his ; the thing was there from
the outset.   And his critical analysis of

---

[1] Acts ii. 44–47, iv. 32–37. It is noteworthy that each of these
accounts of the " Communism " of the primitive Church,
which are thought to emanate from separate sources, is given
as the immediate sequel to an account of the descent of the
Holy Spirit.

" gifts of the Spirit " (1 Cor. xii.–xiv.), which results in giving a relatively low place to abnormal phenomena, and exalting moral and intellectual endowments, and, above all, *agapé*, love or charity, to the highest places, is a genuinely scientific estimate of the situation as it was from the beginning. This does not mean a reduction of the supernatural character of the primitive Christian experience. It is a recognition of the essential quality of the supernatural as revealed in Christ.

The primitive Church, while it enjoyed the fellowship of the Holy Spirit, and appealed to the manifest work of the Spirit (somewhat naïvely conceived) as evidence of the dawn of the new Age, did not reflect upon it. Nor did it embody any clear doctrine of the fellowship in its preaching. Such a doctrine first appears in the epistles of Paul.

Paul had reflected deeply upon the new life realized in the Christian community. It may well be that before his conversion his attention had been arrested by the free, joyful, and enthusiastic fellowship of these sectaries. However that may be, when he became a Christian he fully accepted the belief of the primitive disciples that this new life was a manifestation of the Holy Spirit. The miraculous unity of the fellowship, he believed, was the creation of the Spirit, " for in one Spirit were we all baptized into one body " (1 Cor. xii. 13); and the diversity of gifts, by the same Spirit, were divinely intended as the equipment of members of the

body for function in its life. He also
believed, as is implied in the citation of
prophecy in Acts ii. 17–21, that this life in
the Spirit marked the Church as being the
true " Israel of God " in its final, " eschatological," manifestation (Gal. vi. 15–16).
But his reflection upon this idea led him to
a more profound interpretation of it. In
order to appreciate it we must give some
consideration to the background of the idea.

The idea of a supernatural Messianic
community developed in Jewish prophecy
and apocalypse. We may find it already in
Isaiah's doctrine of the Remnant.

" It shall come to pass, that he that is left
in Zion, and he that remaineth in Jerusalem,
shall be called holy, even everyone that is

written among the living in Jerusalem ;
when the Lord shall have washed away the
filth of the daughters of Zion, and shall have
purged the blood of Jerusalem from the
midst thereof, by the spirit of judgment and
by the spirit of burning.[1]   And the Lord
will create over the whole habitation of
Zion, and over her assemblies, a cloud and
smoke by day and the shining of a flaming
fire [2] by night " (Is. iv. 3–5).

Ezekiel pictures the emergence of this
ideal Israel in the figure of the resurrection
of the dry bones :

" Thus saith the Lord God : Behold I will
open your graves, and cause you to come up
out of your graves, O my people . . . and

[1] Cf. Mt. iii. 7–12, Lk. xii. 49, 2 Thess. i. 8.
[2] Cf. Acts ii. 3, 19.

I will put My spirit into you and ye shall live "[1] (Ezek. xxxvii. 12–14).

In Malachi the Remnant idea appears in a strongly eschatological context :

" Then they that feared the Lord spake one with another ; and the Lord hearkened and heard, and a book of remembrance was written before Him, for them that feared the Lord and that thought upon His name. And they shall be Mine, saith the Lord of hosts, in the day when I act, even a peculiar treasure. . . . For behold the day cometh, it burneth as a furnace, and all that work wickedness shall be stubble ; and the day that cometh shall burn them up, saith the

[1] Cf. Rom. vi. 3–11, vii. 6.

Lord of hosts, that it shall leave them neither root nor branch.   But unto you that fear My name shall the sun of righteousness arise with healing in his wings "[1] (Mal. iii. 16–17, iv. 1–2).

In the Book of Daniel the ideal Israel appears as " the people of the saints of the most High," identified with the " Son of Man " of Daniel's vision, to whom the kingdom is given[2] (vii. 13–14, 22–27).   In the Similitudes of Enoch, the " congregation of the righteous," also called " the elect " and " the holy," appear along with the Elect, Righteous, or Holy One, who is also called the Son of Man.

---

[1] Cf. 2 Cor. iv. 6.
[2] Cf. Rom. v. 17, 1 Cor. vi. 2, 2 Tim. ii. 12 (a "faithful saying," *i.e.* a statement of the faith).

" From the beginning the Son of Man was
   hidden,

And the Most High preserved him in the
   presence of his might,

And revealed him to the elect.

And the congregation of the elect and holy
   shall be sown,

And all the elect shall stand before him
   on that day. . . .

And the Lord of spirits will abide over
   them,

And with that Son of Man shall they eat,[1]

And lie down and rise up for ever and ever.

And they shall have been clothed with
   garments of glory,

And these shall be the garments of life
   from the Lord of Spirits ; [2]

[1] Cf. Lk. xxii. 29–30, Ac. x. 41, 1 Cor. x. 16–17.
[2] Cf. 2 Cor. v. 1–5.

And your garments shall not grow old,

Nor your glory pass away [1] before the Lord

of spirits " (Enoch lxii. 7–8, 14–16).

It is unnecessary to point out how much of the imagery and ideas of such passages as these, which could be greatly multiplied, reappears in various parts of the New Testament.

For Paul, with his strongly eschatological background of thought, the belief that the Church was the " people of the saints of the Most High," now revealed in the last days, carried with it the corollary that all that prophecy and apocalypse had asserted of the supernatural Messianic community was fulfilled in the Church. But the eschatological

[1] Cf. 2 Cor. iii. 12–18.

10

scheme of the apocalypses had been pro-
foundly disturbed by the fact that the Messiah had come and the Kingdom of God had
been revealed, while yet this world continued to exist, and the people of God were
still in the body.   The Messiah indeed had
Himself passed into the eternal order, but
His followers still lived " in the flesh "
(though not " after the flesh").   How, then,
could it be true that the prophecies were fulfilled which spoke of the congregation of the
righteous being transfigured into the glory
of an immortal life ?

Paul found the answer to this question
through a restatement in more thoroughgoing terms of the unity existing between
the Messiah and the Messianic community.
Christ, said the *kerygma*, was Son of God "ac-

cording to the Spirit of holiness." The same
Spirit dwelt in His Church. Thus the "communion of the Holy Spirit" was also "the
communion of the Son of God" (1 Cor. i. 9).
It was not enough to say that Christ, being
exalted to the right hand of God, had
"poured forth" the Spirit. The presence
of the Spirit in the Church *is* the presence of
the Lord : "the Lord is the Spirit" (2 Cor.
iii. 17). Thus the "one body" which the
one Spirit created is the Body of Christ. To
be "in the Spirit" is to be "in Christ,"
that is to say, a member of the Body of
Christ. The personality of Christ receives,
so to speak, an extension in the life of His
Body on earth. Those "saving facts," the
death and resurrection of Christ, are not
merely particular facts of past history, how-

ever decisive in their effect ; they are re-
enacted in the experience of the Church.   If
Christ died to this world, so have the members of His body ; if He has risen into newness of life, so have they ; [1] if He being risen
from the dead, dieth no more, neither do
they ; [2] if God has glorified Him, He has
also glorified them.[3]   They are righteous,
holy, glorious, immortal, according to the
prophecies, with the righteousness, holiness,
glory, and immortality which are His in full
reality, and are theirs in the communion of
His Body—" in Christ."

This is the basis of Paul's so-called
" Christ-mysticism."   It is noteworthy that
as his interest in the speedy advent of Christ
declines, as it demonstrably does after the

[1] Rom. vi. 4.   [2] Rom. vi. 8–9.   [3] Rom. viii. 29–30.

time when he wrote 1 Corinthians,[1] the
" futurist eschatology " of his earlier phase
is replaced by this " Christ-mysticism." The
hope of glory yet to come remains as a background of thought, but the foreground is
more and more occupied by the contempla-
tion of all the riches of divine grace enjoyed
here and now by those who are in Christ
Jesus. " Blessed be the God and Father of
our Lord Jesus, who has blessed us with
every spiritual blessing in the heavenly
places in Christ ! " (Eph. i. 3).

This was the true solution of the problem
presented to the Church by the disappoint-
ment of its naïve expectation that the Lord
would immediately appear ; not the restless

[1] See my article, " The Mind of Paul : Change and
Development," in the *Bulletin of the John Rylands Library*, vol.
18, no. 1.

and impatient straining after signs of His coming which turned faith into fantasy and enthusiasm into fanaticism; but a fuller realization of all the depths and heights of the supernatural life here and now. The prayer of the Church as taught by Paul was no longer, " Let grace come and let this world pass away. O Lord, Come ! "[1] but " to be strengthened by His Spirit in the inner man; that Christ may dwell in your hearts by faith; that ye being rooted and grounded in love, may be strong to apprehend with all saints what is the breadth and length and depth and height, and to know the love of Christ that passeth knowledge, that ye may be filled unto all the fulness of God " (Eph. iii. 16–19).

[1] *Didaché*, x. 6.

This transformation of eschatology into mysticism (if that is the right word) had consequences in the practical sphere. That there is a certain tension or even contradiction between eschatology and ethics has often been observed. It is indeed possible to defend eschatology on the charge of being non-ethical. No doubt the thought of judgment to come may provide a powerful motive, and the exhortation to watch and pray lest the Day come upon you like a thief in the night is never altogether out of place. But an exclusive concentration of attention upon glory to come, with the corresponding devaluation of the present, its duties and opportunities, its social claims and satisfactions, obscures the finer and more humane aspects of morality. We have already

noticed how lamentably the outlook of the
Revelation of John falls below the ethical
ideals of the Gospel.   Now, in the epistles of
Paul the doctrine of the Church as the Body
of Christ, the sphere of divine grace and of
supernatural life, is the foundation for a
strong, positive, and constructive social
ethic, which develops in a remarkable way
the ethical teaching of Jesus.

If Christ lives in His Church, then love
shown to the brethren is a part of that
communion with Christ which is life eternal.
" Be of one mind ; have the same love.
Do nothing in strife or vainglory, but in
lowliness of mind think each other better
than yourselves. Do not seek your own
ends, but one another's. In a word, have
the same thoughts among yourselves as you

have in your communion with Christ Jesus,[1]
who being in the form of God humbled
Himself and became obedient even unto
death ; for which reason God exalted Him
and gave Him the name above every name "
(Phil. ii. 3 *sqq.*). Here we have ethics
developing directly out of " Christ-mysticism." It is noteworthy that while Paul's
reflection upon the saving facts of the death
and resurrection of Christ leads him to the
love of God as the supreme principle exhibited in these facts, it is his reflection upon
the Spirit and the *charismata* or gifts of the
Spirit in the Church that leads him to love
or charity as at once the greatest of all
charismata—" the love of God shed abroad

---

[1] This translation, which follows that of Erich Haupt in
Meyer's Commentary, seems to me to give the correct sense
of this difficult sentence. The current rendering does violence
to the Greek.

in our hearts by the Holy Spirit given to us " (Rom. v. 5)—and the root principle of all morality.[1] The true supernatural life, now brought into being by Christ, is the life distinguished by the " fruits of the Spirit " as described in Gal. v. 20, and exhibiting the dispositions set forth in the hymn of charity in 1 Cor. xiii.

It is in the epistles of Paul, therefore, that full justice is done for the first time to the principle of " realized eschatology " which is vital to the whole *kerygma*. That supernatural order of life which the apocalyptists had predicted in times of pure fantasy is now described as an actual fact of experience. In its final form, it is true, the consummation

[1] See my article, " The Ethics of the Pauline Epistles," in *The Evolution of Ethics*, edited by Hershey Sneath (Yale University Press, 1927), pp. 308–312.

of life is still a matter of hope, but the earnest (*arrhabon*) of the inheritance is a present possession; and an *arrhabon* is a sample of goods guaranteed to be of the same kind and quality as the main consignment. In masterly fashion Paul has claimed the whole territory of the Church's life as the field of the eschatological miracle.

In the Fourth Gospel the crudely eschatological elements in the *kerygma* are quite refined away. It is true that the eschatological outlook survives in the anticipation of a Day when those who are in the tombs will hear the voice of the Son of God, and come forth to the resurrection of life or of judgment (v. 28-29). But the evangelist points out with emphasis that this is not the resurrection to which the Gospel primarily refers. "I know," says Martha, "that he will rise at the resurrection on the Last Day"; and Jesus replies, "I am the resurrection and the life. . . . He who is alive and believes on me will never die" (xi. 24–26). That is to say, eternal life is a present and permanent possession of believers in Christ. Again, in the farewell discourse Jesus is made to promise that He will "come again," but it is made clear that this promise of a second coming is realized in the presence of the Paraclete, the Holy Spirit, in the life of the Church (xiv. 16–19, xvi. 12–16). The evangelist, therefore, is deliberately subordinating the "futurist" element in the eschatology of the early Church to the "realized eschatology" which, as I have tried to show, was from the first the distinctive and controlling factor in the *kerygma*. His theme is life eternal, that is to say, in eschatological language, the life of the Age to Come, but life eternal as realized here and now through the presence of Christ by His Spirit in the Church.

The fact is that in this Gospel even more fully than in Paul, eschatology is sublimated into a distinctive kind of mysticism. Its underlying philosophy, like that of the Epistle to the Hebrews, is of a Platonic cast, which is always congenial to the mystical outlook. The ultimate reality, instead of being, as in Jewish apocalyptic, figured as the last term in the historical series, is conceived as an eternal order of being, of which the phenomenal order in history is the shadow or symbol. This eternal order is the Kingdom of God, into which Christians have been born again, by water and the Spirit (iii. 3–8). That is to say, life is for them fully real ; they are nurtured by the *real* Bread and abide in the *real* Vine. This is the Johannine equivalent for the primitive Christian declaration that the age of fulfilment has dawned, or the Pauline declaration that if any man is in Christ there is a new creation. Its organic relation to primitive eschatological conceptions can be illustrated in various ways.

In prophecy the promise of the future was associated with the knowledge or vision of God. When Jeremiah speaks of the new covenant by which the true Israel of the future shall be constituted, he gives as its outstanding feature, "They shall all know Me,

from the least of them unto the greatest of
them, saith the Lord " (xxxi. 34). Again, in
Is. lii, " Awake, awake, put on thy strength,
O Zion ; put on thy beautiful garments, O
Jerusalem ! Ye were sold for nought, and
ye shall be redeemed without money.
Therefore My people shall know My name :
They shall know in that day that I am He." [1]
The significance of such declarations becomes clearer when we observe that while
the prophets repeatedly speak of the knowledge which God has of His people, their
knowledge of God is almost always the object of prayer, aspiration, command, or
promise. Ideally, Israel knows God as
God knows him ; but actually such know-

---

[1] This " I am He " of the Deutero-Isaiah becomes in the
Fourth Gospel the solemn affirmation of the finality of Christ :
viii. 28, xiii. 19.

ledge is, in any full sense, reserved for the glorious future. The Fourth Evangelist takes up the idea, and declares that now, as never before, authentic knowledge of God is available for men in union with Christ, the Son who knows the Father as He is known by Him ; and such knowledge is eternal life.[1]

Here the language of the Fourth Gospel approximates to that of contemporary Hellenistic mysticism, which taught that by *gnosis* man might enter into union with God, and so become divine and immortal. It seems clear that the evangelist's intention was to reinterpret the Christian Gospel in terms agreeable to the most elevated kind of religious experience, outside Christianity, with which he was acquainted, recognizing

[1] Jn. x. 15, xvii. 3.

that in it there was something of the light that lighteneth every man that cometh into the world.

But it would be a mistake to suppose that the Johannine doctrine of eternal life through knowledge of God is merely a variety of the current teaching of Hellenistic mysticism. The knowledge of God of which the evangelist speaks is a function of the Christian fellowship. As Paul recognized in the Christian Church the marks of the supernatural Messianic community, in so far as it was the Body of Christ, so John teaches that knowledge of God and eternal life are enjoyed by those who are united to Christ. To be united to Christ means to be the object of His love in laying down His life for His friends, and in return to love

11

Him, to trust and obey Him, and to love all those who belong to Him.[1]   This divine love was the power which in Christ brought eternal life within reach: " God so loved the world that He gave His only Son that whosoever believeth in Him should not perish, but have everlasting life " (iii. 16). This agrees with the Pauline interpretation of the character of the supernatural life given to the Church: God commended His love in that Christ died for us, and that love is shed abroad in our hearts through the Holy Spirit.

We can hardly call this anything but mysticism, but it is mysticism with a difference.   It arises directly out of the primitive Christian valuation of the facts of history and

[1] John x. 11–15, xv. 13–17, xiv. 23–24, xiii. 34–35.

experience as eschatological facts, that is, as the ultimate manifestation in time of the eternal counsel of God.

John, however, takes a step beyond Paul. Paul, as we have seen, derives from the eschatological valuation of the Church's life in the Spirit a " Christ-mysticism " which represents a conclusive reinterpretation of eschatology; and he also presents the death and resurrection of Jesus in their full meaning as eschatological facts. But of the life of Jesus he makes little except as preparation for His death. Here the Synoptic Gospels do more justice to that part of the *kerygma* which recited the facts of the life of Jesus as an integral element in the eschatological process. Now for John the whole life of Jesus is in the fullest sense a revelation of

His glory.　What was true of Christ's work in the Church after His resurrection was already true of His words and works in the flesh.　By them, as truly as by His death and resurrection, He brought life and light into the world.　John therefore draws together two separate strains in the development of Christian thought : that which started from an eschatological valuation of the facts of present experience, and that which started from a similar valuation of the facts of past history.　Accordingly, he has given to his work the form of a " Gospel," that is to say, of a restatement of the *kerygma* in historical terms.

In the Fourth Gospel we can discern, no less clearly than in Mark, and even more clearly than in Matthew and Luke, the fixed outline of the historical section of the *kerygma* as we have it in Acts x and xiii : the ministry of John the Baptist, the " a-nointing " of Jesus with the Holy Spirit, His teaching and works of mercy and power in Galilee ; His ministry in Judæa and Jerusa-lem, His arrest and trial before Pilate, His crucifixion, burial, and resurrection.

The close affinity of the Fourth Gospel with the apostolic Preaching will become plainer if we attempt an analysis of it some-what on the lines of our analysis of Mark.

The theme of " fulfilment," which in Mark is represented by the citations of prophecy with which the Gospel begins, is in John represented by the Logos doctrine of the Prologue. Whatever else the Johan-nine Logos may be, it is on one side of it the

Word of the Lord, by which the heavens were made ; which in the prophets came to His own, and His own received it not. The Prologue represents this Word of the Lord as the Light which, shining in the darkness, stage by stage grows in intensity to the point at which all its rays are focused on one spot of blinding glory in the Incarnation. For the background of the idea we might cite such prophetic passages as Is. lx, which speaks of the ideal Israel of the future : " The Lord shall be unto thee an everlasting light, and thy God thy glory " (lx. 19). The same symbolism recurs everywhere in the apocalypses. It is not simply that the prophets spoke words which now at last found their verification in the great divine event. It is that this event is the emergence into full operation of

that very Word which in past history strug-
gled for utterance.   This is surely a more
profound rendering of the idea of the fulfilment of prophecy.

The evangelist next records, in traditional
manner, the ministry of John the Baptist.
His function, as in Mark, is to bear testimony
to the coming of the Messiah, and in
particular to the fact that He will " baptize
with Holy Spirit."   In order to do this the
Messiah is, again as in Mark, Himself
" anointed " with Holy Spirit.   To this also
the Baptist bears witness.   The theme of the
testimony to Christ is here expanded by the
addition of several further witnesses, who
apply to Him the traditional eschatological
title—Messiah, Son of God, King of
Israel.   At last Jesus Himself speaks, and

claims for Himself, as in Mark, the most mysterious and august of all these titles, " Son of Man " (i. 51).

There now follow, as in Mark, stories of the miracles of Jesus, accompanied by discourses which explain their meaning in the light of the Johannine " sublimated eschatology." The miracle of Cana speaks of the coming of that new order which is to the old as wine to water. The cleansing of the Temple foreshadows the new Temple which is the Body of Christ (ii. 21). In the healings at Cana and Bethesda Christ gives life, as in the healing of the blind at Siloam He gives light. In the Feeding of the Multitude the bread is interpreted by the help of the symbol of the manna, which had in Jewish tradition come to stand for the spiritual food of the Age to Come. Christ is in fact giving to the world the " real bread," which conveys eternal life. That the bread is Himself is agreeable to the experience of the Church that in the " communion of the Holy Spirit," which constituted the new life, it enjoyed the presence of the Lord.

The record is interspersed with sayings which emphasize the truth that in this historical ministry of Jesus " the time is fulfilled and the Kingdom of God has drawn near." Thus, " Do you not say, Four months, and then the harvest comes ? " (The harvest is an old prophetic symbol.) "I say to you, lift up your eyes and behold the fields : they are already white for harvest " (iv. 35). Again, " The hour is coming, and *now is*, when true worshippers will worship the Father in spirit and in truth " (iv. 23). " The hour is coming, *and now is*, when the dead will hear the voice of the Son of God, and those who hear will come to life " (v. 25). And this latter saying receives illustration on the grand scale in the story of the raising of Lazarus, which exhibits Christ as " the resurrection and the life," through whom eternal life is a present possession, and no longer a hope for the " last day."

Like Mark again, John traces in the ministry that growing opposition to Jesus which led to His death. But he gives to it a more profound interpretation. Since with Christ the eternal light has come into the world, to sin against the light is to be judged. And this is in fact the " last judgment " of which prophecy and apocalypse spoke, and which, if the coming of Christ is indeed the fulfilment of prophecy, must have taken place when He came. " This is the judgment : that the Light has come into the world, and men loved darkness rather than light " (iii. 19). Hence, when the opposition has reached its height, and Jesus stands in prospect of death, He can declare, " *Now* is the judgment of this world ; *now* is the prince of this world cast out" (xii. 31). It is a more pointed and even more logical statement of the Pauline doctrine that in the death of Jesus God condemned sin in the flesh and triumphed over principalities and powers. The eschatological idea of judgment has received a conclusive reinterpretation.

As we approach the narrative of the

Passion, the place of the Apocalyptic Discourse in Mark is taken by the discourse in the Upper Room.   In this discourse, as we have seen, the prediction of the second advent of Christ is interpreted in the sense of His presence in the Church through His Spirit.   The Passion itself is set forth as the event in which Christ is more fully " glorified " than in any of His words or works (xii. 23–33), because on the one hand it is the most complete revelation of His love for His friends, and on the other hand it is, as the *kerygma* had insisted from an early date, the means by which He finally effected the salvation of man.   " For their sakes I sanctify myself, that they also may be sanctified in reality " (xvii. 19).   In these words the " holiness," that is, the super-

natural character, of the Messianic community is directly related to the saving fact
of the death of Christ. The last words of
His earthly life are " It is finished " (xix. 30).
They are an impressive statement of the conviction that in the life and death of Jesus the
whole counsel of God is fulfilled, as the
eschatological valuation of these facts had
implied from the beginning.

Finally, the resurrection is recorded, as in
the other Gospels, and in agreement with
the form of the *kerygma*. But in the Fourth
Gospel it is not so much a new act in the
drama of redemption, for the victory of
Christ is already complete, and His glory
already manifested in His life and death.
It is narrated as the sign which seals for the
disciples the reality of that which He has

accomplished, and the finality of His Person : " Thomas said, My Lord and my God ! " (xx. 28.)

In this profound restatement of the apostolic Preaching the Fourth Evangelist has succeeded in bringing into one picture those elements which in its earlier forms appear as past, present, and future. On the one hand all that the Church hoped for in the second coming of Christ is already given in its present experience of Christ through the Spirit; and on the other hand this present experience penetrates the record of the events that brought it into being, and reveals their deepest significance. " The Word was made flesh, and dwelt among us, and we beheld His glory." All the sense of finality that eschatology strove to express is in that amazing declaration, which is at once a comprehensive summary of the life of Jesus, and contains in itself all that the highest hopes of man can aspire to ; for beyond the vision of God we cannot aspire.

The work of Paul and John represents the most significant and far-reaching developments of the apostolic Preaching in the New Testament.   As we have seen, their writings, as well as those of other New Testament writers, betray a direct acquaintance with the traditional forms of the *kerygma*.   We could not otherwise account for the way in which they all recur to certain guiding ideas, and even certain arrangements of these ideas, and formulæ for expressing them.   The primitive *kerygma* lived on.

As the Church produced a settled

organization of its life, the content of the *kerygma* entered into the Rule of Faith, which is recognized by the theologians of the second and third centuries as the pre-supposition of Christian theology. Out of the Rule of Faith in turn the Creeds emerged. The so-called Apostles' Creed in particular still betrays in its form and language its direct descent from the primitive apostolic Preaching.

At the same time, the *kerygma* exerted a controlling influence upon the shaping of the Liturgy. While theology advanced from the positions established by Paul and John, the form and language of the Church's worship adhered more closely to the forms of the *kerygma*. It is perhaps in some parts of the great liturgies of the Church that we are still in most direct contact with the original apostolic Preaching.

In this survey of the apostolic Preaching and its developments two facts have come into view : first, that within the New Testament there is an immense range of variety in the interpretation that is given to the *kerygma* ; and, secondly, that in all such interpretation the essential elements of the original *kerygma* are steadily kept in view. Indeed, the farther we move from the primitive modes of expression, the more decisively is the central purport of it affirmed. With all the diversity of the New Testament writings, they form a unity in their proclamation of the one Gospel. At a former stage of criticism, the study of the New Testament was vitalized by the recognition

12

of the individuality of its various writers and their teachings. The results of this analytical stage of criticism are of permanent value. With these results in mind, we can now do fuller justice to the rich many-sidedness of the central Gospel which is expressed in the whole. The present task of New Testament criticism, as it seems to me, is the task of synthesis. Perhaps, however, "synthesis" is not quite the right word, for it may imply the creation of unity out of originally diverse elements. But in the New Testament the unity is original. We have to explore, by a comparative study of the several writings, the common faith which evoked them, and which they aimed at interpreting to an ever-widening public.

It is this task which I have tried to plot

out in these lectures. It should be evident
that there is room for a great deal of investigation at every point. Work which has
been done during the present century, and
particularly since the War, has provided us
with fresh standpoints, and with fresh
illustrative material. There are new methods
of Gospel-criticism, and there is an almost
bewildering mass of material supplied by the
comparative study of religion in and about
the New Testament period, from Jewish,
Hellenistic, and Oriental sources. Indeed,
it has sometimes seemed as if the study of
Pauline and Johannine thought, in particular, might resolve itself into a study of
religious eclecticism. But as we master this
mass of material, instead of being mastered
by it, it will enable us to define more pre-

cisely the meaning of the terms employed by these teachers, and I am convinced that the result will be to bring into more startlingly clear relief the fundamental Christian message which Paul and John proclaim in fresh and invigorating forms.

There is one further part of the task, to which in these lectures I have done no more than allude, and that is, to ascertain the relation between the apostolic Preaching and that of Jesus Christ Himself. I have said something about it elsewhere.[1] I will here only state my belief that it will be found that the primitive *kerygma* arises directly out of the teaching of Jesus about the Kingdom of God and all that hangs upon it ; but that it does only partial justice to the range and

[1] In *The Parables of the Kingdom* (Nisbet, 1935).

depth of His teaching, and needs the Pauline and Johannine interpretations before it fully rises to the height of the great argument.   It is in the Fourth Gospel, which in form and expression, as probably in date, stands farthest from the original tradition of the teaching, that we have the most penetrating exposition of its central meaning.

In conclusion, I would offer some brief reflections upon the relation of this discussion to the preaching of Christianity in our own time.

What do we mean by preaching the Gospel ?   At various times and in different circles the Gospel has been identified with this or that element in the general complex of ideas broadly called Christian ; with the promise of immortality, with a particular theory of the Atonement, with the idea of " the fatherhood of God and the brotherhood of man," and so forth. What the Gospel was, historically speaking, at the beginning, and during the New Testament period, I hope these lectures have in some measure defined. No Christian of the first century had any doubt what it was, or any doubt of its relevance to human need. How far can it be preached in the twentieth century ?

A well-known New Testament scholar has expressed the opinion that " the modern man does not believe in any form of salvation known to ancient Christianity." [1] It is indeed clear that the primitive formulation of the Gospel in eschatological terms is as

[1] Kirsopp Lake, *Landmarks of Early Christianity*, p. 77.

strange as it could well be to our minds. It
is no wonder that it has taken a long time,
and stirred up much controversy, to reach
the frank conclusion that the preaching of
the early Church, and of Jesus Himself, had
its being in this strange world of thought.
For many years we strove against this conclusion. We tried to believe that criticism
could prune away from the New Testament
those elements in it which seemed to us
fantastic, and leave us with an original
" essence of Christianity," to which the
modern man could say, " This is what I have
always thought." But the attempt has
failed. At the centre of it all lies this alien,
eschatological Gospel, completely out of
touch, as it seems, with our ways of
thought.

But perhaps it was not much less out of touch with the thought of the Hellenistic world to which the earliest missionaries appealed. Paul at least found that the Gospel had in it an element of " foolishness " and " scandal " for his public. But he and others succeeded in reinterpreting it to their contemporaries in terms which made its essential relevance and truth clear to their minds. It is this process of reinterpretation that we have been studying. Some similar process is clearly demanded of the preachers of the Gospel in our time. If the primitive " eschatological " Gospel is remote from our thought, there is much in Paul and John which as it stands is almost equally remote, and their reinterpretations, profound and conclusive though they are, do not absolve us from our task.

But the attempt at reinterpretation is always in danger of becoming something quite different; that which Paul called, "preaching another Jesus and another Gospel." [1] We have seen that the great thinkers of the New Testament period, while they worked out bold, even daring ways of restating the original Gospel, were so possessed by its fundamental convictions that their restatements are true to its first intention. Under all variations of form, they continued to affirm that in the events out of which the Christian Church arose there was a conclusive act of God, who in them visited and redeemed His people; and

[1] 2 Cor. xi. 4, Gal. i. 6.

that in the corporate experience of the
Church itself there was revealed a new quality
of life, arising out of what God had done,
which in turn corroborated the value set
upon the facts.

The real problem for the student of the
New Testament is not whether this or that
incident in the life of Jesus is credibly
reported, this or that saying rightly attributed to Him; nor yet whether such and
such a doctrine in Paul or John can be
derived from Judaism or the " mystery-
religions." It is, whether the fundamental
affirmations of the apostolic Preaching are
true and relevant. We cannot answer this
question without understanding the Preaching, nor understand it without painstaking
study of material which in some of its forms

is strange and elusive ; but without answering this question, we cannot confidently claim the name of Christian for that which we preach.   To select from the New Testament certain passages which seem to have a " modern " ring, and to declare that these represent the " permanent element " in it, is not necessarily to preach the Gospel.   It is, moreover, easy to be mistaken, on a superficial reading, about the true meaning of passages which may strike us as congenial. Some of them may not be as " modern " as they sound.   The discipline of confronting the Gospel of primitive Christianity, in those forms of statement which are least congenial to the modern mind, compels us to rethink, not only the Gospel, but our own prepossessions.

It is for this reason that I conceive the study of the New Testament, from the standpoint I have indicated, to be of extreme importance just now. I do not suggest that the crude early formulation of the Gospel is our exclusive standard. It is only in the light of its development all through the New Testament that we learn how much is implied in it. But I would urge that the study of the Synoptic Gospels should be more than an exercise in the historical critic's art of fixing the irreducible minimum of bare fact in the record; and that the study of Paul and John should be more than either a problem in Comparative Religion or the first chapter in a History of Dogma. Gospels and epistles alike offer a field of study in which the labour of criticism and interpretation may initiate us into the " many-sided wisdom " which was contained in the apostolic Preaching, and make us free to declare it in contemporary terms to our own age.

APPENDIX

Eschatology and History

Eschatology and History

THOSE WRITINGS OF the Old Testament which we are accustomed to call the historical books are in the Jewish Canon reckoned among the prophets ; and rightly so.   One of the direct results of the work of the prophets of the eighth and seventh centuries B.C. was an outburst of historical composition.   Other Oriental peoples had for a long time produced chronicles, which have a high value as a record of events. But the corpus of historical writings which runs from the Book of Joshua to the Second Book of Kings, and indeed includes also the narrative parts of the Pentateuch, is something different from a chronicle of events. It exhibits history as a unity, with a meaning which makes sense of all its parts. As Dr. Clement Webb has recently put it, " The ' historical element ' in the Old Testament is already, in intention and profession, not a mere collection of stories, but a history of the world, although no doubt a history of the world told from a special point of view and with a practical intent." [1]

The principle which gives unity and meaning to the whole is the idea of the moral government of the world by a divine providence, which manifests itself in divers parts and divers manners in the successive episodes of the experience of the people of

[1] *The Historical Element in Religion* (Allen & Unwin, 1935), pp. 39–40.

God, and is working towards the fulfilment of a divine purpose.

But while recorded history is the field within which the divine purpose is being worked out, it can never be said, in the prophetic view, that recorded history fully reveals the purpose of God. This revelation will not be given until the last term in the historical series has come into view— the Day of the Lord. It is only prophetic foresight of the Day of the Lord that makes it possible to see the whole of history as divinely governed. It seems probable that the idea of the Day of the Lord is a part of primitive Hebrew mythology. Certainly it is older than the earliest of the prophets whose works we possess. But if so, we must suppose that in popular mythology the idea stood for an unconditioned and unrelated catastrophe, supervening incalculably upon the course of history. The prophets strenuously endeavoured to give to the idea an ethical and rational meaning, by relating it to the course of events in the past and to the tendencies of the present. It was thus not simply one more detached event, though of a different order, but the consummation of the whole series of events.

To prophecy succeeded apocalypse. It works with the prophetic scheme of history, but with certain differences. In particular, it virtually gives up the attempt to recognize divine meaning in the present. The mighty hand of the Lord is to be seen in events of the remote past, and will again be seen in the future, but in the present the power of evil obscures it. This does not mean that events have escaped the divine control. " The Most High ruleth in the kingdom of men," but His rule is hidden. This change of perspective, which can be sufficiently accounted for by the prolonged subjection and sufferings of the faithful, serves to give greater emphasis to the belief, which, as we have seen, was also the belief of the prophets, that only in the Day of the Lord will the divine meaning and purpose of history come to light.

At the same time, the radical contrast of " this age " and " the age to come," which now begins to be expressed, serves to bring out the supra-historical character of the Day of the Lord. If on one side it is an event—the last term in the series of events—on the other side it is not an event in history at all ; for it is described in terms which remove it from the conditions of time and space. In one sense this is no doubt a reversion to the pre-prophetic mythology ; but again it brings into bold relief an essential character of the idea, which it bears even in the prophets. The *eschaton*, even though it may be conceived in terms of the devastation of Israel by Assyria, or, again, of a glorious return of Judah from Babylonian exile, is never simply one event following upon another, as the giving of the Law followed upon the Exodus, or the Return upon the Babylonian Captivity, only with the difference that no further event will follow upon it in turn. It is such that no other event either could follow or need

follow upon it, because in it the whole purpose of God is revealed and fulfilled.

In prophecy and apocalypse alike, the
divine event, the *eschaton*, is always " round
the corner." The prophet never conceives
himself as standing midway in the course of
history, surveying the past through its centuries of change, and foreseeing the future
through a similar series of changes. It is
not true that either prophets or apocalyptists
write, in this sense, "reversed history," or an
imaginary narrative of a future course of
events, like Mr. Shaw or Mr. Wells.

The idea that they do so is an illusion
based upon two facts. First, later exegesis
found the "fulfilment" of prophecy in a
series of events, often covering a long span
of time. Although we have disavowed

such exegesis, its ghost may still haunt us. Secondly, the apocalypses are frequently attributed to personages who lived long before the actual composition of the books, and who are represented as surveying the *actual* course of history through centuries, in the guise of predictions. Although we recognize the fiction for what it is, it is not easy wholly to escape its effects on the mind.

Actually the prophet foresees one thing only, the Day of the Lord, the *eschaton*. This statement needs to be qualified only so far, that some prophets or apocalyptists emphasize the nearness in time of the *eschaton* by giving a turn to contemporary events, such that they melt, after a brief development, into the mythical or supernatural traits of the Day of the Lord. In the *eschaton* is concentrated the whole meaning which, *if* history were to go on, might be diffused throughout a long process. In this sense the prophetic view may be said to "foreshorten" history; for so it appears to us, who know that many centuries elapsed after the debacle of Judah in 586 B.C., or the Seleucid persecution of 168 B.C., which were the immediate prelude to the End, for Jeremiah and for the author of Daniel respectively.

In reality time-measurement is irrelevant here. An absolute end to history, whether it be conceived as coming soon or late, is no more than a fiction designed to express the reality of teleology within history. If the maxim " *Die Welt-*

geschichte ist das Weltgericht" is to be maintained in its full sense, then there must somehow be in history an element of finality. If, as Solon said, a man may not be pronounced happy until he is dead, or as Aristotle put it, happiness can be predicated only of a " complete life," then similarly the significance of history can be estimated only when history is over and can be looked at as a closed whole. It is this that is symbolized in the myth of the Last Judgment, the End of the World. Since no man has ever experienced the end of history, it can be expressed only in the form of fantasy.

When our modern apocalyptists set forth the Shape of Things to Come, their imaginative skill is used to produce a fictitious narrative which *looks* so like history as we know it that we almost forget that it has no closer relation to actuality than the vision of Jewish apocalyptists. The form of forecasting a process rather than a single event laden with meaning does not alter the fact that we are dealing with symbol and not with actuality, in the one case as in the other. The time-scale is irrelevant to that which has never received embodiment in the forms of time and space, and therefore has no existence in the temporal order. Where the prophets chiefly differ from our modern writers about the future is not so much in predicting an *early* end of the world, but in clothing the coming event in forms which do not properly belong to time at all, but to eternity. They thereby imply that the teleology of history is not purely immanent, but is determined by the purpose of a God who transcends the temporal order.

We may now consider more closely the character attributed to the Day of the Lord.

It is in the first place supernatural. Not, indeed, that the supernatural factor is absent from any part of history, for in the prophetic view all history is the field of divine action. But the *eschaton* is manifestly supernatural. The hidden rule of God in history is revealed. " Then His Kingdom shall *appear* throughout all His creation " (Assumption of Moses, x. 1). After long centuries of waiting, mankind shall *see* the glory of the Lord.

Secondly, since the will of God is absolute right, the Day of the Lord will be the overthrow of the powers of evil, and judgment upon the sin of men.

Thirdly, since the will of God for man is perfection of life in His image and in fellowship with Him, the Day of the Lord will bring to those in whom His will is fulfilled a new life which is both glorious and endless.

In all these respects, the Day of the Lord is the " fulfilment " of history. While it belongs, in the last resort, to the realm of the " wholly other," it is nevertheless not something alien and unrelated to the recorded course of events. For history depends for its meaning and reality upon that which is other than history. The real, inward, and eternal meaning, striving for expression in the course of history, is completely expressed in the *eschaton*, which is therefore

organically related to history. Nevertheless, it is unique and unlike any other event,
because it is final. It is not as though the
Creator had arbitrarily fixed a certain date as
the "zero-hour" of His world, so that events
which might conceivably have followed it
are not permitted to happen. It is such
that nothing more *could* happen in history,
because the eternal meaning which gives
reality to history is now exhausted. To conceive any further event on the plane of
history would be like drawing a cheque on
a closed account.

At the same time the Day of the Lord is
not the end of things in the sense that it
negates the values inherent in history, so
that it might be conceived as a kind of
Nirvana or holy nothingness, in which the

illusions of the time-process are finally laid to rest. On the contrary, the values implicit in history are here fully affirmed. They are not destroyed but sublimated. The Day of the Lord brings with it new heavens and a new earth, and transforms human nature into the likeness of " the angels of God." Thus the *eschaton*, or ultimate, is also a beginning. It is the end of history, but the beginning of " the Age to Come," which is not history but the pure realization of those values which our empirical life in time partly affirms and partly seems to deny. Inevitably, the only way in which this can be described is in imagery of a sensuous type, which often gives the appearance of being a crude materialism. For example, one of the most common images is that of the heavenly banquet.   But some at least of the apocalyptists surely knew that the Kingdom of God is not eating and drinking, but righteousness, peace, and joy ; that is, it is the pure reality which we partly apprehend in the most exalted moments of our human experience in time.

In the New Testament the apocalyptic symbolism of the Old recurs freely, but with a profound difference.   The divine event is declared to have happened.   Consider the following propositions, taken from all parts of the New Testament :

" The Kingdom of God has come upon you "
    (Matt. xii. 28).
" This is that which was spoken by the
    prophet " (Acts ii. 16).

" If any man is in Christ, there is a new
creation " (2 Cor. v. 17).

" He has rescued us out of the dominion of
darkness and transferred us into the
Kingdom of the Son of His Love "
(Col. i. 13).

" We are being transfigured from glory to
glory " (2 Cor. iii. 18).

" He has saved us by the washing of rebirth
and the renewal of the Holy Spirit "
(Titus iii. 5).

" Having tasted the powers of the Age to
Come " (Heb. vi. 5).

" Born again, not of corruptible seed, but of
incorruptible " (1 Pet. i. 23).

" The darkness is passing, and the real light
is already shining . . . it is the last
hour " (1 John ii. 8).

14

From these and many similar passages it is surely clear that, for the New Testament writers in general, the *eschaton* has entered history; the hidden rule of God has been revealed; the Age to Come has come. The Gospel of primitive Christianity is a Gospel of realized eschatology.

In other words, a particular historical crisis, constituted by the ministry, the death, and the resurrection of Jesus Christ, is interpreted in terms of a mythological concept, which had been made by the prophets into a sublime symbol for the divine meaning and purpose of history in its fullness. The characteristics of the Day of the Lord as described in prophecy and apocalypse are boldly transferred to the historical crisis.

First, it is fulfilment. " The time is fulfilled " is the declaration which Mark inscribes over the whole Gospel record. Similarly, Paul declares, " When the fullness of time had come, God sent forth His Son." The frequent appeals to the fulfilment of prophecy, which the modern reader is apt to find tedious and unconvincing, are a piecemeal assertion of the one great fact that the meaning of history is now summed up. We mistake them if we suppose that the writers would have been equally interested in *any* prediction of *any* casual event which happened to be fulfilled. That which the prophets foresaw was the Day of the Lord, and that alone. The fulfilment of prophecy means that the Day has dawned.

Secondly, the supernatural has manifestly entered history. The arm of the Lord is made bare. "The blind see, the lame walk, lepers are cleansed and the deaf hear, the dead are raised, and to the poor good tidings are proclaimed." The miracle-stories of the Gospels correspond closely with the symbols which the prophets had used to depict the supernatural character of the Age to Come. They may be regarded, once again, as a piecemeal assertion of the one great fact that with the appearance of Christ the age of miracle arrived.[1] The story of His ministry is told as a realized apocalypse.

Thirdly, this open manifestation of the power of God is the overthrow of the powers of evil. " If I by the finger of God cast out demons, then the Kingdom of God has come upon you," says Jesus in the Synoptic

[1] See my article, " Miracles in the Gospels," in *Expository Times*, vol. xliv, no. 11, pp. 504 *sqq.*

Gospels.   The Christ of the Fourth Gospel, on the eve of His death, declares, " Now is the prince of this world cast out."   Paul says that in the Cross God triumphed over principalities and powers.   The theme recurs in other parts of the New Testament.

Fourthly, this is the judgment of the world.   In the death of Christ, says Paul, God manifested His righteousness and condemned sin in the flesh.   " This " (according to the Fourth Gospel) " is the judgment, that the Light has come into the world (with the incarnation of the Word), and men loved darkness rather than light."

Finally, eternal life, the " Life of the Age to Come," is now realized in experience. Christ is risen from the dead, the firstfruits of them that sleep, and we are raised with

Him in newness of life. He who believes *has* life eternal.

I have done no more than offer a few pointers towards a conclusion which must be clear to all who study the New Testament with the language and ideas of Jewish eschatology in mind, the conclusion that the writers have deliberately, boldly, and consistently applied those ideas and that language to the facts of the ministry, the death, and the resurrection of Jesus Christ. The implication is that in those facts all that the prophets meant by the Day of the Lord is realized. There is here a divine event, unique and decisive, in which the whole purpose of God in history is made manifest.

Naturally, when a conception hitherto

belonging to the realm of mythology is declared to be realized in history, it is itself remoulded by the facts. How far the fantastic imagery of apocalyptic was taken literally by its authors or readers, it will perhaps always remain impossible to say. But when that imagery is applied to actual facts, its symbolic character becomes plain, and some elements in it are tacitly dropped as inappropriate. Thus the apocalyptic picture of the darkening of the sun and the collapse of the material universe is not taken up, except in the greatly reduced form of a supernatural darkness and an earthquake, represented as accompanying the crucifixion and resurrection of the Lord ; and the clouds upon which the Messiah was to descend to judgment appear only as a subordinate element in the scenes of the Transfiguration and the Ascension. But when all allowance is made, it remains that the New Testament writers intend with full seriousness to represent the coming of Christ as the unique divine event to which prophecy and apocalyptic referred.

One change necessarily follows when the divine event passes from the realm of mythology to the realm of history. While its character of finality remains, in the sense that it is decisive, it can no longer be final in the sense that nothing can happen after it. For it is in the nature of our time-experience that it cannot be bounded either before or after. It is, indeed, in this sense that time is, as Plato said, the " moving image of eternity." Hence, any event within history, forming part of the time-series, must be followed by other events. And so the coming of Christ was followed by a further historical period. But the New Testament writers are clear that history is henceforward qualitatively different from what it was before Christ's coming.

Indeed, they exploit that aspect of the Day of the Lord in which it was not only the *eschaton*, regarded from the point of view of previous history, but also the beginning of a new order, superior to the historical. Paul goes so far as to say that in Christ we are dead to the world, that is to say, to the historical order, and that God has raised us together with Christ, and made us to reside with Him in the heavenly places. True, this new life is secret.   On the empirical plane we still live the earthly life; but though we live " in the flesh," we no longer live " after the flesh."   " You are dead, and your life is hid with Christ in God " (Col. iii. 3).   Thus no conception of Christianity as a religion is fully true to the New Testament which does not recognize that the " Christian Era," as we call it, marks an abrupt break in the relation in which the people of God, and, indeed, the whole human race, stands to the historical order.

" For the end of the world was long ago,
    And all we dwell to-day
   As children of some second birth,
   Like a strange people left on earth
    After a judgment day."

This view of the historical status of the events comprised in the coming of Christ introduces us at once to what Professor Gerhard Kittel, in *Mysterium Christi*, calls " *das Ärgernis der Einmaligkeit*," " the scandal of particularity." How can we now take seriously a view which selects one particular episode in history, and declares that it possesses an absolute and final quality distinguishing it from all other events ?

Now with particularity, as such, many historians have no quarrel—those at least who with Troeltsch regard their science as " idiographic " rather than " nomothetic." Mr. H. G. Wood, in his recent Hulsean Lectures, *Christianity and the Nature of History*, distinguishes the two types of science thus :

" The one concerned with the discovery of fruitful general principles, the other with the appreciation of particulars whose nature cannot be fully explained by general laws; the one interested in particular facts for the sake of discovering the general laws, the other interested in general laws for the sake of appreciating individuality and value; the one concerned with the phenomena of repetition, the other with the unique and non-repeatable elements of experience : the one best represented by physics, and the other best represented by history " (p. xxxvii).

Mr. Wood goes on to argue that the specific character of the particular events which are the subject of history is that they are " productive of significant change." Of an event which is " historic " in the full sense one must be able to say, " First, this having happened, things can never be the same again. We cannot revert to the *status quo ante*. Second, this having happened, it never can happen again. No exact repetition is desirable or even possible" (p. 11).

If we take this view of history, as against the " evolutionary " view, then there is no longer any objection in principle to the doctrine that the coming of Christ is in the highest degree such an " historic " event, unrepeatable and productive of significant change. But the Christian claim seems to go beyond this. It is, that this episode in history is unique in a sense which is not,

and could not, be true of any other event.
" Once for all at the consummation of the
ages He was manifested "(Heb. ix. 26).　Such
a statement cannot, of course, be regarded
as a scientific induction from observed facts.
It is of the nature of a religious intuition or
act of faith.　Nevertheless, it may be that
such an intuition does after all provide the
clue to the meaning of history.

I shall here refer to an already famous
passage in the first volume of Professor
Arnold Toynbee's massive *Study of History*.[1]
The author is seeking for an adequate cause
for the rise of civilization.　After investigat-
ing the evolutionary factors of Race and
Environment, he pronounces that he has
" drawn a blank."　One discovery only has

[1] The passage to which I refer is in Vol. I, pp. 271 *sqq.*

emerged—" The cause of civilizations is not simple but multiple ; it is not an entity but a relation.   We have the choice " (he proceeds) " of conceiving this relation either as an interaction between two inhuman forces . . . or as an encounter between two superhuman personalities." He chooses the latter alternative, following Plato's lead and turning from the formulæ of science to mythology.

" An encounter between two superhuman personalities," he observes, " is the plot of some of the greatest stories and dramas that the human imagination has conceived.   An encounter between Yahweh and the Serpent is the plot of the story of the Fall of Man in the Book of Genesis ; a second encounter between the same antagonists . . . is the plot of the New Testament, which tells the story of the Redemption ; an encounter between the Lord and Satan is the plot of the Book of Job ; an encounter between the Lord and Mephistopheles is the plot of Goethe's *Faust* ; an encounter between Gods and Demons is the plot of the Scandinavian *Voluspà* ; an encounter between Artemis and Aphrodite is the plot of Euripides' *Hippolytus.*"

The theme of the plot, Professor Toynbee shows, is in all cases covered by the formula, " Challenge and Response," and this formula furnishes him with the desired clue to the rise of civilizations. With this aspect of the matter we are not at present concerned. But we must observe that this great encounter is in most cases (he says in all cases, but I do

not think this is strictly true) conceived as a
unique event.   In particular, " in the New
Testament the uniqueness of the divine
event is of the essence of the story ; and
this has been a stumbling-block to the
Western intellect ever since the geocentric
conception of the material universe was first
impugned by the discoveries of our modern
Western Astronomy."   But by an appeal to
Sir James Jeans's theory of the origin of the
planetary system he deftly turns the flank of
the astronomical attack.   " In this portrayal
of the encounter between two stars which is
supposed to have led to the appearance of
Life on Earth, the rarity and the momentous-
ness of the event turn out to be almost as
much of the essence of the story as they are
in the Book of Genesis and in the New

15

Testament." Thus the " scandal of particularity " is not avoided by modern science
any more than by Christian theology.

In his application of the myth of the great
encounter, Professor Toynbee abandons the
idea of strict uniqueness, for he assumes that
a specific episode of " Challenge and Response " led to the rise of each of the civilizations known to history. But if the universal
myth is to be taken as testifying to a valid
spiritual intuition of something deeply embedded in the structure of the universe, as
he assumes, then it is significant that ideally
it speaks of an absolutely unique event. In
the history of civilizations the great encounter is not unique but extremely rare,
but this rarity must be taken as what Plato
might have called a " shadow " or " image "

of the idea of uniqueness which is the ultimate reality in the case, as the virtue of a good man is only a shadow of the Idea of the Good.

Christianity, however, as Professor Toynbee recognizes, holds to the strict uniqueness of the divine event. Further, the Christian form of the Myth is the only one that even professes to have been embodied in an historical event—the only one, unless one should include the astronomical theory of the primæval assault upon the Sun, out of which the planetary system and life itself emerged; for to the lay mind it is never quite clear whether the astronomers, like other physicists, suppose themselves to be describing actual facts, or to be offering a symbolic myth which helps us to visualize

imaginatively the results of their mathe-
matical calculations.   In any case, Christianity insists that in the death of Jesus *sub
Pontio Pilato* there took place a unique encounter between God and the powers of
evil out of which a new kind of life for
mankind emerged.

In making this claim we are not, I think,
altogether outside the scope of Professor
Toynbee's application of the myth.   He
holds that each civilization arose out of an
episode of challenge-and-response which
for that civilization is unique and final in its
results.   It is not unique absolutely, only
because civilization itself is not a single
phenomenon but a multiple one.   But in
relation to any one particular civilization he
postulates an event possessing the same

qualities of uniqueness and finality which Christianity attributes to the coming of Christ. This event is so momentous, and in the last resort so mysterious and so little to be accounted for by immanent evolutionary factors, that it cannot be adequately presented except in the mythical form of an encounter between superhuman personalities. And yet, be it observed, this event actually happened, at a date which can in most cases be fixed within a century or two.

I suggest that if we are thinking not of civilizations but of religion, the element of multiplicity may well disappear. Religions, indeed, that is to say, the forms and institutions in which they are embodied, are many, and may be included among the constituent factors in the various civilizations known to history. Religion, however, is one. Indeed, it may well turn out that the unity underlying all varieties of civilization can ultimately be expressed only in terms of religion, as the relation established between the human spirit and its total environment, material, physical, and spiritual. (That there is such an ideal unity of civilization seems to be implied in Professor Toynbee's argument about the "comparability of facts," and in his treatment of the several historical civilizations as species of a genus.) The Christian claim, then, implies that the clue to the meaning of history in its religious aspect lies in the historical episode of the coming of Christ, which can be adequately interpreted only as a drama of superhuman personalities, and is as such unique.

While, however, the New Testament

affirms with full seriousness that the great divine event has happened, there remains a residue of eschatology which is not exhausted in the " realized eschatology " of the Gospel, namely, the element of sheer finality.   While history still goes on, a view of the world, which, like the prophetic and Christian view, insists that history is a unity, must necessarily represent it as having an end, as well as a beginning, however impossible it may be for philosophy to admit the idea of finite time.   Thus the idea of a second coming of Christ appears along with the emphatic assertion that His coming in history satisfies all the conditions of the eschatological event, *except* that of absolute finality.

We must be clear just how much is

implied in this idea. It would not be true to say that in the New Testament as a whole (whatever may be true of possible isolated passages) the ministry, death, and resurrection of Christ are regarded as merely provisional, or as anything short of the unique and absolute entrance of the Kingdom of God, the *eschaton*, into human experience. " The Word was made flesh " : no more absolute relation of God to history than that can be conceived.

The true nature of the *geminus adventus* of the Lord can best be studied in the Sacrament of the Eucharist, in which the spiritual consciousness of the Church is most intense. The Eucharist was from the beginning an eschatological sacrament, an anticipation of that heavenly banquet which was the august and mysterious symbol of the perfection of life in the Age to Come. Its eschatological character is most clearly and emphatically preserved in the Eastern liturgies, though the Western liturgies (Roman and Anglican) have not altogether missed it. It was also, from a very early date—at least from the time when Paul " received " the tradition which he " delivered " to the Corinthians in A.D. 50—a commemoration of the death of the Lord " under Pontius Pilate," i.e. of the historical facts in which the Church saw a " realized eschatology." It is the focus of what Dr. Webb has called, in his recent book, the " memory " of the community, by which the events of the past are attested as realities essential to its life.[1] At the same time it

[1] *The Historical Element in Religion*, pp. 84 *sqq*.

has been, again from the time of Paul at latest, and we may suppose from those early days in which " He was known to them in the breaking of bread," a sacrament of the very presence of Christ in and with His people.   Past, present, and future are indissolubly united in the sacrament.   It may be regarded as a dramatization of the advent of the Lord, which is *at once* His remembered coming in humiliation and His desired coming in glory, both realized in His true presence in the Sacrament.

In the Eucharist, therefore, the Church perpetually reconstitutes the crisis in which the Kingdom of God came in history.   It never gets beyond this.   At each Eucharist we are *there*—we are in the night in which He was betrayed, at Golgotha, before the empty tomb on Easter day, and in the upper room where He appeared ; *and* we are at the moment of His coming, with angels and archangels and all the company of heaven, in the twinkling of an eye at the last trump. Sacramental communion is not a purely mystical experience, to which history, as embodied in the form and matter of the Sacrament, would be in the last resort irrelevant ; it is bound up with a corporate memory of real events. History has been taken up into the supra-historical, without ceasing to be history.

I believe that if we consider all that this implies, we are led some way towards a distinctively Christian conception of the nature of history.

There are two opposing views of history

which have been widely held by those who would think it " unscientific " to take account of the spiritual factor. Either history is a chapter of accidents, or it is an evolutionary process. Religion can, in theory, come to terms with either view. If, as in some Eastern religions, the whole order of space and time is relegated to the sphere of illusion, then religion is well content to abandon history as at bottom senseless, and to turn to the eternal order in a " flight of the alone to the Alone." In the West, however, in recent times, an optimistic and idealistic type of religion has made terms with the evolutionary view of history. It has assumed that the direction of change in the process is of the nature of " progress," and it has introduced the spiritual factor by a doctrine of immanence, according to which the supposed law of progress is identified with the activity of the divine Spirit. In its Christian form it has often attempted to reinterpret eschatology in terms of an evolutionary teleology. The Kingdom of God is identified with a Utopian goal of social evolution upon earth, and the magnificent affirmations of faith in its coming have been buttressed by a professedly scientific theory of the inevitability of progress.

The evolutionary doctrine of progress has been the object of searching criticism in recent years. With it I will not concern myself here. But if the argument of this paper is sound, the theological form of that doctrine to which I have referred betrays a misconception of the nature of Christian eschatology. The Kingdom of God is not Utopia. The Gospel does not speak of " progress," but of dying and rising again. The pattern of history is revealed less in evolution than in crisis. Once in the course of the ages the spirit of man was confronted, within history, with the eternal God in His kingdom, power, and glory, and that in a final and absolute sense. There was a great encounter, a challenge and response, a death and resurrection ; and divine judgment and life eternal came into human experience.

By that supreme crisis the meaning of all history is controlled. As it is reconstituted, by faith, in the experience of successive individuals and generations of mankind, the inward reality of history is revealed. The divine challenge reaches the soul of man. For his response to the challenge, positive or negative, and for its immediate consequences, he must bear responsibility, for good or ill; and the nature of his response may shape the conditions of the next crisis. The whole course of history, however, remains plastic to the will of God. This world of things, persons, and events can never forfeit, because of human sin, its one title to reality —namely, its fitness to mediate the call of God to man. For it has once been the field upon which the great encounter was fought to a decision, and it bears the mark of that encounter for ever.

Beyond the proximate effects of his choice the mind of man cannot foresee. He can never forecast the shape of things to come, except in symbolic myth. The true prophet always foreshortens the future, because he, of all men, discerns in history the eternal issues which lie within *and yet beyond it*. The least inadequate myth of the goal of history is that which moulds itself upon the great divine event of the past, known in its concrete actuality, and depicts its final issue in a form which brings time to an end and places man in eternity—the second Coming of the Lord, the Last Judgment.